Concerned Intervention

When Your Loved One Won't Quit Alcohol or Drugs

JOHN & PAT O'NEILL

NEW HARBINGER PUBLICATIONS, INC.

Copyright 1993 by John and Pat O'Neill
New Harbinger Publications, Inc.
5674 Shattuck Avenue
Oakland, CA 94609

Cover design by SHELBY DESIGNS AND ILLUSTRATES
Illustrations by Mike Krone

Library of congress catalog number: 92-061813
ISBN 1-879237-36-9 Paperback
ISBN 1-879237-37-7 Hardcover

An earlier version of this book was published under the title *Help to Get Help*, by Creative Assistance Press, Austin, Texas. Copyright 1989, distributed by Texas Monthly Press, Inc.

Distributed in the U.S.A. by Publishers Group West; in Canada by Raincoast Books; in Great Britain by Airlift Book Company, Ltd.; in South Africa by Real Books, Ltd.; in Australia by Boobook; and in New Zealand by Tandem Press.

00   99   98

10   9   8   7   6   5   4

To our adult children, Catherine, Julie, John Jr., and Dan, with love and gratitude for all they have taught us.

And to the late Donald E. Hunter, who, as an Air Force chaplain, first helped our family to get help.

Contents

Part One: Getting Started

The Usual Starting Point • Is Alcohol (or Another
Drug) Really the Problem? • How Can I Tell? • Are
They Really Hooked? • How Can I Confront When I
Use Alcohol/Drugs Myself? • How Can I Help If He
Won't Admit There Is a Problem? • Does the Help
Really Work? • Chemical Dependency—C.D.

"Let It Begin With Me" • The One You Love Is on
Booze or Drugs • More Than Dick and Jane Families
• Co-Dependency—Another Name for Survival
• How Does It Happen? • Silent Fears • What's
Real? • Who Buried My Feelings? • "I Am Not
Angry!!!" • Isn't Mom Wonderful! • Children of
Silence • Beware of Powerlessness • A First Step
• Who Hits Bottom? • What Price Secrecy?
• Getting Started • Just How Serious Is This? • A
Special Word to Parents • A Road Now Well-Traveled

Caution: The Usual Help...May Not! • How Bad Is It?
• Beware the Professional Enabler • Where to Turn
• So for Now, Be Careful • Far Too Many • Shining
Examples • C.D. Is a Specialty

Part Two: Taking Action

What Does It Take? • There Is a High Road •
Recovery Planning • Six Critical Actions • 1. Seek
Accurate, Current Information • 2. Arrange a

About the Authors

John and Pat O'Neill are human relations training consultants based in Austin, Texas. They have worked with over 200 companies and agencies and have presented seminars and workshops to over 80,000 people.

The O'Neills are Licensed Chemical Dependency Counselors and National Certified Addiction Counselors who have worked as a husband-wife counseling team since 1973. They trained at the Johnson Institute in Minneapolis and have since studied and worked with many of the top names in the field. They were among those who pioneered the concepts of concerned person intervention and family treatment.

Over the past fifteen years John and Pat have served as consultants to many Fortune 500 companies, the U.S. Armed Forces, numerous other government agencies, as well as national treatment organizations. They have developed ongoing community information presentations, designed and managed employee assistance programs, and helped organize alcohol and drug abuse education programs at all educational levels.

Though possessing considerable clinical experience, the O'Neills see their mission as advocates for families suffering from alcoholism and related diseases. Their special focus is educating the public about effective intervention methods and quality treatment and advocating for addictive disease research. John and Pat are frequent media guests and popular presenters at regional and national gatherings.

Their book, *Concerned Intervention*, is a guide to family recovery from chemical dependency and co-dependency. The book is based on lessons learned from their experience with hundreds of families seeking intervention, counseling, and treatment. Special emphasis is placed on ways to identity healthy, properly trained professional counselors, affordable patient-centered treatment, and compatible self-help groups.

Acknowledgments

Concerned Intervention summarizes two decades of learning from thousands of people who have touched our personal and professional lives. We thank each of them for their love, support, encouragement. and most of all for the pushes, shoves, and nudges that kept us on the path.

We are also grateful for the legacy of the pioneering professionals who discovered these practical and direct routes to wellness. Until their efforts, the road to recovery was a faint and winding trail through a wilderness of public apathy and professional indifference. But today, thanks to them, the roadway is clearly illuminated by the glow of community awareness and the light of new medical and mental health interest.

Gratitude and respect to mentors and professional peers, too numerous to possibly mention, who, in spite of the frustrations and pain, continue in their commitment to help families overcome this disease.

Thanks to our families of origin, who may not always have understood our mission but have respected and supported our work.

Introduction

Through the years we have worked with hundreds of suffering families and friends of alcoholic or otherwise chemically dependent persons. We have presented educational programs to thousands more, many of whom have shared their stories with us. Two facts have become increasingly clear. First, there is a well-defined and proven sequence of specific choices and actions that mark the road most individuals and families follow on the way to intervention and recovery. And second, if caution is not used, there is potential for many expensive, time-consuming—even deadly—detours and cul-de-sacs on the route. So this book is about staying on a proven path and avoiding the hazards along the way.

Families and friends of chemically dependent persons need practical answers to these questions: What has happened? Why my family, friend, or co-worker? What can I do about it? To whom should I turn? Whom can I trust? Where will I find the courage and support to take action? Why is quality help for alcohol and other drug problems often illusive? How can I avoid misguided excursions in the quest for recovery? Our folklore about these matters is full of harmful myths. But, worse yet, until recently there was hardly any validated information in school curriculums at any level—especially in the universities. For most people, no matter how otherwise well-educated and informed they might be, these questions require updated answers. There are now many excellent books available on the separate subjects of alcoholism and drug abuse, family systems, intervention, and treatment. But there was not a complete, easy-to-apply, self-contained basic training manual for the personal war on drugs that begins when someone important to you becomes harmfully dependent on mood-altering chemicals and you are hurting. We wrote *Concerned Intervention* to meet that need by pointing out a clear, straight, proven path to intervention, treatment, and recovery.

Concerned Intervention is about tragedy, turmoil, and trouble. Yet it is a hopeful book full of facts that lead to understanding and positive change, with suggestions that the reader can use—right now—to reach out for effective, affordable, approachable help. Our intended reader is the family member, friend, co-worker, or employer who is trying to deal with someone else's drinking or drugging problem. But we believe that executives and managers at all levels, schoolteachers, counselors and administrators, and judges and law enforcement officials will also find the information helpful in their work. Certainly, if we had our way, every physician, clergy person, marriage counselor, psychologist, and social worker would hand a copy of the book to almost all their clients. For the evidence is growing by the day that most, yes most, of the people seen by such helping professionals are experiencing illnesses, dysfunctions, and relationship breakdowns because of an underlying alcohol or drug problem—either in themselves or someone they love.

This is not a theoretical work. We are not scholars. We are experienced-in-the-trenches alcohol and drug abuse counselors.

Concerned Intervention is based on our firsthand experience and the legacy of the pioneering professionals who discovered these practical and direct routes to wellness. Until their efforts, the road to recovery was a faint and winding trail through a wilderness of public apathy and professional indifference. But today, thanks to them, the roadway is clearly illuminated by the glow of community awareness and the light of new medical and mental health interest. We believe that our extensive personal and professional experience in the application of these principles can also make a contribution, especially because of our somewhat unique role as a counseling couple.

The book is divided into four parts: "Getting Started," "Taking Action," "Understanding the Problem," and "Finding the Resources." The four parts track with the questions uppermost in the minds of most readers: Should I act? What should I do? Why should I do it? Where can I get the help I need? The chapters in each part are essentially self-contained. In fact, each could be a separate booklet on its particular subject. This compartmentalization required some repetition among chapters. But this resulted in a more reader-friendly, functional, and easy-to-use book. By referring to the chapter descriptions in the Table of Contents or to the Index, readers will be able to quickly locate the information they need.

Finally, *Concerned Intervention* is a book about pain—why it happens and how to make it go away. It is said that there are no guarantees in life. Maybe so. But we know this. When suffering people have come to accept the ideas synthesized here and followed the courses of action suggested, lives change for the better, people get well, families mend, and the pain goes away.

Perhaps earlier sincere but unsuccessful efforts to find help have you feeling confused, frustrated, and disillusioned. Maybe you've chosen or been sent into blind canyons, unmarked detours, and deadends in the search for a straight path to recovery. Unquestionably, many genuinely concerned people, truly wanting to take right action and willing to accept professional guidance, often pay a shocking price in time, money, and emotional pain for help that doesn't help. In some cases the "professional" assistance has even caused real harm.

Still, in spite of the many valid reasons for fear, doubt, and hesitation, there is even more basis for hope. For it has been our special privilege to view the renewed personhood, restored health, and revived love that blooms in the happier place that lies beyond this stormy disease. The thousands of families who have found or rediscovered such wellness testify to the possibilities of recovery for you and your family. Their proven success, collective strength, and genuine willingness to help you along the way are powerful and realistic reasons for hope and confidence. It is a happy truth that today thousands are winning the family battle against alcohol and drugs. Their victories show that, armed with basic information, equipped with proven guidelines, connected to the right help resources, and encouraged by the support of those who have gone before, you and your loved ones don't have to hurt anymore.

Maybe you're thinking, "This sounds too easy. They don't understand. Our situation is a lot more complicated than all this sounds." Be warned that perhaps the greatest barrier to recovery is clinging to the idea that your situation is so different that what worked for others will not work for you. To view a chemically dependent person or your particular situation as unique is to sentence him or her and you to continued suffering. It is only by accepting the idea that you are dealing with a universal illness—one that responds to proven interventions and treatments—that recovery can begin. And such is truly the case.

As the title implies, this is a help book. So use it in any way that will help. There are four parts. "Getting Started" does just that; it gives reasons why you need to get moving and how to avoid harmful directions. "Taking Action" suggests specific, proven intervention and treatment steps and offers guidelines on how to recognize quality help. "Understanding the Problem" provides an optimistic update on today's national effort to understand, prevent, and remedy alcoholism and other drug dependencies. "Finding the Resources" deals with where to turn and how to pay the costs involved, and lists specific help resources nationwide as well as recommended reading.

The four parts encompass thirteen chapters. In addition, each major paragraph has a headline summarizing its content, so you can jump from topic to topic if need be. In a crisis scan the Index at the end of the book to locate immediate, helpful information. By all these means, *Concerned Intervention* is designed to be very reader-friendly and immediately useful. So skip around all you want. We think the organization is logical and the book is best read from front to back. But this disease is not always logical. Accordingly, read what seems important at the moment and come back for the rest later. In other words, do whatever it takes to find the help you need. The idea is to provide *Concerned Intervention*.

Concerned Intervention

Part One

Getting Started

1

Straight Answers to Key Questions

Nothing in life can prepare us for the storms that a chemical obsession unleashes within a family or group of friends. The auto accidents, arrests, breakups, batterings, and bankruptcies; the ruined plans and shattered dreams; the heartache and bewilderment—these things really do happen. Even if conditions are not that bad, as alcohol or other drugs gain more and more control, the emotional connections within the family begin to disintegrate. And that's disaster enough. There is great and growing pain when once-loving relationships turn into tortured contests for survival. We know this to be true from personal experience and many years of interacting professionally with families and other groups of concerned persons being torn apart by alcohol and drug problems. Still, if someone you care about has a problem with alcohol or other drugs, there is hope. There is help. It does work. Here is how to find it.

If you are trying to live or work with someone who has a serious alcohol or other drug problem, such optimism may ring hollow. Yes! You are right. There are no quick, magic solutions. But if you will trust the real-life experiences of people just like yourself, be willing to open-mindedly consider some useful facts, and risk a few new and different choices, there is a way out.

Let's get started!

The Usual
Starting Point

This book is primarily for those trying to deal with somebody else's alcohol or drug problem. In our experience most want answers to these three key questions before they feel right about taking action:

1. Is alcohol (or some other drug) truly the primary problem?

2. How do I justify confronting someone else if I drink or drug myself?

3. Is it really possible to help when he or she won't admit there is a problem?

Is Alcohol (or Another Drug)
Really the Problem?

How can you tell, with certainty, if someone you care about has become dependent on alcohol or other drugs? What's the difference between acceptable use of mood-altering chemicals, abuse of these substances, and the pathology called chemical dependency? How do you know that the person is not just being bad, stupid, or crazy—or all three? These questions are frequently asked by family members and other concerned persons who are living or working with a person who is experiencing life problems as a result of drinking or drugging.

Suspect the Obvious

Very few people live part of their life as good, intelligent, sane people and then start acting bad, stupid, and/or crazy unless alcohol and drugs are the culprit. So when we see behavior changes in those we love, we should first suspect and investigate the obvious. Certainly there are emotional and psychiatric illnesses. And occasionally people will turn morally sour. But such dysfunctions are relatively rare. Alcohol and drug-related problems, on the other hand, are encountered in one of every three American families. If someone you care about is acting in ways that concern you and there is reason to believe he or she drinks or drugs, look at that issue first. You will probably save a lot of time, heartache, and money by doing so. Even if there are underlying physical and emotional problems, those conditions cannot be dealt with until the alcohol or drug use is first addressed. Chemical dependencies are always primary.

How Can I Tell?

Clearly, there is a difference between a groom toasting his bride with a single glass of fine champagne and the skid row drunk trying to get his shaking hands on a pint of cheap muscatel. Or between the postsurgical patient taking pain killers for a few days and the chronic heroin addict willing to rob or even kill for a fix. But just where along the line between these extremes are the points that distinguish between acceptable use, harmful abuse, and pathological "ism"?

Use/Abuse/Dependency

The following definitions may be useful:

Use   Legal mood-altering chemicals consumed
                 by choice, in safe amounts, at appropriate
                 times and places, in ways not harmful to
                 self or others.

Abuse   Mood-altering chemicals *still being used by
                 choice*, but in unsafe amounts, or at inappro-
                 priate times and places, or in ways harmful
                 to self or others.

Dependency Powerlessness over mood-altering chemi-
                 cals characterized by episodes of loss of
                 control and/or the apparent inability to
                 modify drinking and drugging even after
                 experiencing negative consequences. Some-
                 times but not always accompanied by phys-
                 ical addiction to the chemical. Dependency
                 may or may not be preceded in life by a
                 history of abuse.

Are They Really Hooked?

How can you tell if someone has crossed the line and become dependent? First of all, the fact that you're reading this information
makes it a very real possibility. Being concerned enough to want
to read this book is a strong indication of how many clues you're
picking up. But if there is doubt in your mind, here is a simple
quiz. Answer the questions on the basis of your observations of
the person about whom you are concerned.

1. Does he/she do things under the influence of alcohol and/
   or other drugs that violate his/her own rules for behavior?

2. Does he/she break promises to himself/herself about the
   use of alcohol and/or other drugs?

3. Is he/she paying an emotional price (shame, guilt, fear, re-morse, self-directed anger, etc.) for using alcohol and/or other drugs?

4. Does he/she seem to have a different version of his/her own drinking/drugging behavior than witnesses?

5. In your opinion, would he/she become defensive, ration-alize, or even lie if you asked him/her these questions?

(From here on, for convenience, we will most often use mas-culine pronouns. But everything said applies to both sexes. Chemi-cal dependencies are definitely equal opportunity diseases.)

If you think that the person about whom you are concerned would have failed this quiz, there are two possible explanations. Either he is deliberately choosing to abuse chemicals in the face of adverse consequences—a highly unlikely case—or he has become dependent on chemicals and is sick and in need of help. If his sick-ness is causing you pain, you may find it helpful to learn more about the nature of this illness so you can take positive steps to intervene.

Chapters 9 through 11 contain more detailed information about alcoholism and other drug dependencies. But, assuming a crisis led you to this book, there may not be time or the inclination to read all that information now. For the time being, we suggest the following attitude toward someone who appears hooked on alcohol or another drug: they are sick. They have a pathology in every sense of the word. The mainstream scientific consensus is that alcoholism and other chemical dependencies are physiological diseases with a powerful genetic component. This is a most unique pathology, however, because it surrounds itself with an array of emotional and behavioral symptoms that make it difficult to diag-nose, hard to intervene upon, and demanding of highly specialized long-term treatment and aftercare. Such a view is, beyond all else, extremely practical because those who approach this malady with that picture in mind are usually successful in bringing about change in the situation. Those who choose to moralize, analyze, or chastise tend to stay stuck in their pain. So, if you want to stop hurting, approach this disease like any other disease. Such an attitude will get results.

How Can I Confront When I Use Alcohol/Drugs Myself?

Maybe you can't! If chemicals are causing a serious problem in your life, then you yourself are probably chemically dependent. In such a case the only way you could help someone else is to say, "I'm going for help. Why don't you come along?" But, assuming your own use is under control, you can certainly be a help to others. To be effective, however, you will need to take these steps:

1. First, deal with the ways the other person's drinking/drugging has affected you.

MOM &
DAD   →2. Stop doing things that enable that person to escape the consequences of drinking/drugging.

3. Learn how to confront the behavior without attacking the person.

4. Become familiar with help options that can be accepted without loss of dignity.

Making those changes in your relationship with the chemically dependent person will place you in a posture of love and concern. And love and concern gives you a right to try to help. Thus, if the person says something like "Where do you get off talking to me about alcohol? You drink as much as I do!" the simple response is "Because I care about you and am concerned."

Caution: Personal Experience Need Not Apply

There is another caution regarding our own use of alcohol/ drugs. Most of us form strong opinions on the subject from our own experiences. Many readers will have, at some time or other, abused alcohol or other mood-alterers and thus, in certain respects, believe they "understand" the problem. But there is a trap to the idea of using your own drinking or drugging experience in dealing with someone else's. If you are like the vast majority of temporary alcohol and drug abusers, you were probably able to learn from the negative physical, behavioral, and emotional consequences and modify your use with willpower and reason. Since you were able to change your drinking and/or drug use as the result of such "Wow! I'll never do that again" experiences, it's easy to conclude that everyone else ought to be able to do likewise, especially when the victim is someone you love and respect. But that's the trap. Not everyone else can.

Your personal experiences notwithstanding, there is blended into our drug-using/abusing culture a significant and tragic minority of people who permanently lose control over alcohol and other drugs. These people become pathologically dependent not because they are evil, ignorant, or insane but because of a complex and far-reaching disease process. It is complex because it affects every area of the victim's life and far-reaching because it causes pain in the lives of family members, friends, and even co-workers. So any approach to a loved one about an alcohol and/or other drug problem should be tempered by awareness that our own experience with chemicals may not apply and our own pain may even distort reality and block appropriate action. And of course, as mentioned before, there is always the possibility that we are chemically dependent ourselves and are in as much denial as the person about whom we are concerned.

How Can I Help If He Won't Admit There Is a Problem?

Few people are able to break out of a chemical dependency without help. Most who do recover follow a strikingly similar path. First, some significant event or person(s) intervenes and helps them to see the reality of their condition. This new awareness generates a willingness to accept outside help. Then the outside help is successful in getting them to accept their powerlessness, inspiring them to clear away the wreckage of the past and develop new and positive programs for alcohol- and drug-free living.

There are many respected contemporary theories about alcoholism and other chemical dependencies, just as there are a number of plausible models through which to view the family impact of these addictions. Some of these concepts make more sense than others. But, as yet, there is insufficient evidence to prove any of them conclusively. What is important and beyond theoretical controversy is the readily observable truth that some victims of alcohol and drug dependencies die and others get well. Those who recover are the fortunate few who had loved ones caring enough or hurting enough to reach out for help. Recovery is almost always the result of "outside interference." The momentous tragedy of this disease is that it first destroys love, and the resulting unloved victim—helpless from within and abandoned from without—dies. Yes, it is possible to intervene, but your assistance is crucial.

Does the Help Really Work?

Until the 1970s, the only readily available sources of assistance were self-help programs such as Alcoholics Anonymous, based on the renowned Twelve Steps. Such programs were literally lifesavers for those willing to admit there was a problem and be open to help. But the unwilling were sentenced to more suffering and, all too often, death.

Over the last twenty years or so, there has been widespread introduction of excellent health-care-based intervention and treatment models that seem better able to reach the unwilling. These programs accelerate recovery, enhance the benefit of twelve-step programs, and also deal more effectively with the physical and emotional aspects of the disease. At the same time, a much clearer understanding of the family impact of chemical dependency has emerged, accompanied by specific therapies to deal with these issues. Alongside these positive developments in treatment has been the outgrowth of innovative and potent intervention methods that facilitate the chemically dependent person's entry into treatment. So, in spite of yet unanswered questions about specific causes and the lack of a single magic remedy, the prognosis for early intervention and lasting recovery is excellent. In fact, it has become a truism that of all the nation's major health problems, chemical dependency is the most treatable. Again, *there is hope because there is help and it does work*. And you can play a vital role.

Chemical Dependency—C.D.

By now you have perhaps recognized the awkwardness of trying to continually refer to "alcoholism and other chemical dependencies" or "alcoholic or otherwise chemically dependent person." Yet today's drug dependency problem has expanded far beyond just alcohol. To simplify this poly-drug situation, the term *chemical dependency* has been coined.

Nowadays, when someone has become harmfully hooked on a mood-altering chemical, including alcohol, the professionals in the field refer to such persons as chemically dependent and call the disease chemical dependency. This is a very useful term that the press and the public would do well to more fully adopt. In fact, the longer the term is used, the more sense it makes.

In the past, the primary drugs of choice—alcohol, marijuana, and heroin—were actually grown as crops and processed almost like food products. Consequently, many people had trouble thinking of addicts to these earthborn substances as chemically dependent. Then along came real "drugs" such as tranquilizers, amphetamines, and laboratory derivatives of cocaine—closer to our general notion of chemicals. In fact, many of today's chemicals of abuse are just that: chemicals. They are not being harvested from the earth but rather are being synthesized in laboratories, legal and illegal. (It is not the least bit unfair to describe distilleries and breweries as laboratories for turning food products into mood-altering drugs.) Thus, the term *chemical dependency*, if anything, has grown more accurate, descriptive, and acceptable as an all-purpose term to describe a pathological dependency on any mood-altering substance. It seems wise to have a standard, agreed-upon name for a disease that has reached epidemic levels in our proliferating drug culture. To encourage greater acceptance and wider use of this term, as well as to keep this book more concise and readable, the victim of chemical dependency will hereafter be referred to as the C.D. person. Similarly, we will refer to the disease as C.D.

Focus

The C.D. experts advise those trying to deal with someone else's drinking or drugging to focus on practical steps and measures in the here and now rather than wasting energy on why it all happened in the there and then. Understanding alone doesn't arrest alcohol and/or other drug problems; choosing to act and getting the help to do so, however, does. So this is a "what works here and now" book. Our aim is to break down this seemingly overwhelming problem into a series of smaller, less intimidating challenges and then provide the pertinent information, clear guidelines, and practical skills to meet them.

A Starting Point

For starters, we suggest the following logic: If someone you love is putting mood-altering chemicals into his body and if doing that is messing up his life and if he either can't or won't change, then he is unquestionably harmfully dependent. If what you're doing to help the situation isn't working and if doing nothing only seems to make things worse, try something else! And if you're going to change strategies, follow the paths that have led to solutions for the most people. Just take it a step at a time and draw courage from the success stories of those who not only made it through this challenge but report being better human beings for having made the journey.

A Touchstone of Power

Consider also that deep emotions are touched when alcohol or other drugs run wild in a family. It may seem at the moment that those negative energies will destroy your loved ones. But there are positive forces at work as well. There is love, concern, and courage still buried within suffering families and friends as well as much dedication among professionals who work in the field. All the emotional energy, professional skill, and moral support you need is out there waiting for you to connect. Thus, we are confident that, if you're willing to reach for help, wellness for you and yours is close at hand.

2

To Families and Friends

"Let It Begin With Me"

As the song suggests, change around us begins with change within us. It is difficult and painfully frustrating to try to help a C.D. person until we first understand and begin repairing the damage the disease has done to us. One of the first things we tell our clients is "You need to put yourself back at the top of your own priority list." There is no way you can help someone else until you first take care of your needs, your pain, your self. So an important part of getting started is gaining an understanding of just why *their* disease is making *you* sick.

The One You Love Is on Booze or Drugs

Your love is rejected. Your help is refused. Your threats are ignored. You do what needs to be done to keep the family together, but much energy is spent hiding feelings and dealing with pain. Trying to uphold the family image by pretending, fixing, and controlling people and situations becomes physically, emotionally, and mentally exhausting. You don't understand what has happened to your once loving family or even where to find a glimmer of hope.

We have worked with lots of people just like you who felt trapped in an intolerable, painful situation and didn't know where to turn. Frequently seeking out traditional helpers such as clergy, physicians, and psychologists, who lacked the specialized skills to really be of value, family members were left with hope dashed, fears reinforced, power untapped, and questions unanswered. Why? How do families work? What happens when this unique disease takes charge? How can you begin to change your situation? What kind of help truly helps?

More Than Dick and Jane Families

Depending upon the situation, you may be wondering whether you are indeed a member of a family. Rest assured, you are. Families are simply groups of individuals tied together with an emotional bond. Families today are more than the traditional "Dick and Jane" family consisting of Mom, Dad, and kids. They appear in many other diverse forms as well. There are extended families composed of stepparents, stepchildren, adopted children, and sometimes other relatives. There are borrowed families, groups of people with whom you can be close and get needs met when your own family is not available. And there are institutional families: those at work, at school, in the military, or even in a treatment facility.

In all these kinds of families an emotional bonding takes place. When that family unit is healthy, the bonding is positive and healthy. But when a disease such as chemical dependency enters the picture, the picture changes. The bonding becomes negative, feelings become buried alive. People feel trapped, unable to see a way out or make healthy choices until and unless they receive better information and guidance, strong emotional support, and sometimes even loving confrontation. Family members become survivors. Moms, dads, sisters, brothers, daughters, sons-in-laws, co-workers, employers, friends—all begin to learn what it takes to survive in a relationship with someone who is chemically dependent. So when we speak of C.D. families, we are referring to any system suffering from the painful effects of chemical dependency.

Co-Dependency—Another Name for Survival

Living in a C.D. family has been likened to being held hostage. When you feel trapped, survival becomes the focus of your life. Unable to be objective or rational, those living with a C.D. person have to develop techniques, behaviors, responses, and defenses in order to survive. There is little doubt that people living in these situations develop their own pathology. What to call this pathology, however, has been the subject of considerable dialogue over the years. The terms *co-alcoholic*, *para-alcoholic*, and *co-dependent* have at one time or another been used to describe someone who has become full of emotional pain and taken on an array of defensive behaviors. Currently, *co-dependency* and *co-dependent* are the most widely used terms to describe this disease and its victims. In our experience, all who have been emotionally bonded with a chemically dependent person suffer some degree of co-dependency. When you have lived, loved, reacted to, and learned how to survive with someone else's chemical dependency, it is impossible to escape co-dependency. You can't be rich enough, smart enough, protected enough, or powerful enough to escape the trauma or avoid the consequences. We are only human, and our humanity is what makes us all vulnerable.

How Does It Happen?

Life in a C.D. family breaks the rules for healthy living. Time after time, promises are broken. People say things they don't mean and don't say what they really mean. The environment becomes a "crazy" place where reality is harder and harder to figure out. Reading minds becomes a necessary skill. You can't trust the people in your system, and you begin to forget what it was like to trust your own reality. Family members desperately want to believe that all will be well, but are disappointed over and over again. Yet they continue to hope, try to give the C.D. person the benefit of the doubt, and, wanting so badly to trust someone, pretend he is as trustworthy as he once was.

The disappointments multiply, the fears and hopes become intermingled, and the pain gets deeper. Consider, for example, the young girl whose dad promises to show up at her school play. She secretly and silently hopes he will be there. Rationally and objectively it is doubtful that he will appear, but C.D. family members are neither rational nor objective about those they love. On the one hand, she wants him there to share her happiness; on the other, she worries that he will show up drunk and humiliate and embarrass her in front of friends. She fears having to make excuses if he never arrives or alibis for his condition if he shows up drunk—all the while wishing that this time will be different.

Family members desperately want to trust: the next party will be fun, Friday's paycheck will go toward bills, tonight's meal will be peaceful, the chores will be done, future promises will be kept, and on and on and on. Trust is so important to family members that they believe in the unbelievable—that the situation will change or simply go away. And through tears, shed and unshed, people who care or once cared about a C.D. person are revolving around him and his drinking/drugging behavior regardless of the fearful consequences to themselves.

Silent Fears

To live in a C.D. family is to live with unspoken fear. Will he be home for dinner? And in what condition? Will there be peace or

battles? Will you be able to study for an important test or be dodg-
ing an abusive parent? Will your C.D. co-worker do his share of
the job or will you have to cover for him? Agonizing concerns such
as these put the family focus on the C.D. person and downgrade
the needs and wants of others.

Coping with unpredictable and aberrant behavior demands so
much time, energy, and concern that the co-dependent persons
have little left for themselves. Being the constant target of blame
chips and chips away at self-esteem and sense of worth. So you
try harder, believing the "craziness" is your fault. No longer do
family members expect honest answers, promises kept, time for
themselves, respect, cooperation, love. *Yet the real craziness is that
the non-C.D. family members are now feeling worthless and accepting
responsibility for the chaos caused by someone else's totally unacceptable
drinking and drugging behavior. Beyond all else, co-dependency is a disease of misplaced responsibility. Its victims stop managing their own lives
in an attempt to control another's.* As a result, all those involved cease
being what they were meant to be and become pathological actors
in a drama of human destruction. Their internal dialogue says,
"Tell me what you want me to be today so that you don't have to
drink and drug, and I'll be it. How do you want me to look? What
do you want me to say and how do you want me to say it? How
do you want me to love you? Who can I have as friends? What
can I do to make it easier for you so that you won't have to drink
or drug?

The struggling players try to manipulate the C.D. person's
drinking or drugging by being, saying, doing, not doing, looking,
loving—in short, behaving—as they think the C.D. person wants,
believing that controlling the environment will bring the miracle
of change. And with that change will come attention, love, and
respect. This obsessive notion that you can change another person's
drinking or drugging by controlling and manipulating is what co-
dependency is all about. Life is driven by the compulsion to meet
the needs of the C.D. person so that he will stop drinking, love
you, respond to you, care for you, and *be a part of your family.* How
sad and how untrue. Real change begins only when someone in
the family has the courage to acknowledge this powerlessness and
reach out for positive help.

What's Real?

Family members find it increasingly difficult to talk to others about what's really happening. And efforts to speak with the C.D. person meet with wrath, denial, hostility, and conflicting versions of reality:

"You're making too much of this!"
"Stop nagging!"
"You're just imagining things."
"It wasn't that bad."

Spouses of alcoholics experience this kind of rebuff so often they think they are losing their minds; they react by screaming and sobbing, even hiding from the C.D. in fear—yet pretending to the rest of the world that everything is O.K. You must be "crazy"! The C.D. person powerfully projects his painful emotions on those closest, seeing his anger, fear, loneliness, and disgust in others. His inadequacy becomes their inadequacy. The house isn't clean enough, the kids aren't quiet enough, the boss isn't fair enough, the weather isn't sunny enough, etc. So you try harder and harder: scrub floors until they shine, hush kids until they whisper, cover up for him at work, and pray for the weather to change. You try everything; yet things get worse as chemical dependency and co-dependency progress.

Your home becomes a house of fear. There may be screaming, name-calling, and even violence, creating recurring terror. You become afraid to risk the wrath of the C.D. person, becoming secretive and not daring to talk about what is really going on. Please note that not all C.D. persons act out with violence, abuse, D.W.I.'s, or job losses. Some just withdraw and gradually abrogate responsibilities as spouses, parents, citizens, and employees. This isolation can be as painful as the fear. But no matter how the C.D. person acts out his illness and reacts to the family—quietly withdrawn or loudly abusive—family members pay the highest emotional cost.

Who Buried My Feelings?

Chemical dependency and co-dependency are diseases of feelings buried alive. When it's not O.K. to feel, feelings get stuffed. Once-positive feelings for the C D. person are often erased or at least superimposed by many negative feelings. You might attempt telling the C.D. about your sadness or anger—how unloved you feel. But someone in pain has little empathy for the pain of others, and the feelings are thrown back in your face. So you stuff your real feelings and start to pretend.

Because there is so much pretense, feelings get all mixed up. Burying negative feelings also puts a lid on positive feelings—the joy, happiness, and love that give meaning to our lives. Unfeeling family members become robot-like creatures, responding from habit, prior conditioning, and stress rather than through thoughtful consideration of reality.

When behavior is automatic and feelings are denied, the body may react in physical illness—recurring migraine headaches, back problems, gastrointestinal problems, and other conditions that won't go away in spite of many trips to the doctor. Seldom will the physician ask about family life or possible alcohol or other drug problems. So...another illness and another, as nothing in your life changes. It's as though your body is crying out, "Pay some attention to the hurt, the anger, the hopelessness I feel!"

"I Am Not Angry!!!"

It's perfectly natural to become very angry when you are being used, abused, and discounted. But showing that anger can have serious, even dangerous consequences for you. Open, honest anger is nearly impossible. Sometimes anger is stored up, exploding in self-defeating ways. A friend became so frustrated with her unresponsive alcoholic husband that she found herself stopping in disbelief just a breath away from shooting him with his own hunting bow and arrow. Most retaliation is less violent and comes in the form of passive-aggressive behaviors such as being late, spending money, not doing things the C.D. person likes to do, or turning the children against him. Co-dependency forms behaviors that violate your own values and deepen the guilt. You buy booze for him with food money, prostitute yourself by having sex with a smelly drunk, lie to cover up and maintain a false family image.

To overcome the guilt, you buy what the kids want instead of what you need, struggling to give them the attention the C.D. person doesn't.

Isn't Mom Wonderful!

Control the kids, run the household, get a job if necessary, and still find time to be "Volunteer of the Year." Has this happened to you? Do you feel worth the time and energy you give others? Do you spend any money on yourself or, at the opposite extreme, try to spend as much as the C.D. person squanders on alcohol? Do you order what you want in a restaurant or what is cheap? How long has it been since you made a choice for yourself? Do you feel deserving of *anything*?

Children of Silence

The children can't talk about what's really happening, either. When they try to talk to Mom and Dad, they often find themselves targets of angry frustration. If the parent is a C.D., he will either pay no attention, strike out, or switch behaviors. Or, one youngster complained, "He is either buying me a football or kicking me around the house. I don't know what to expect." The other parent, preoccupied with the desperation of the moment, can't hear what the children are saying or respond to their needs. The non-C.D. parent may even insist that everything is alright when the children see that it isn't. Under these stresses, children lose trust in their parents, become fearful, and feel guilty and unwanted. Children sense being torn apart when parents try to get them to take sides. They may hesitate to talk to their sisters or brothers, thinking the other kids don't know what's going on. Older siblings may in fact tell the younger ones that nothing is wrong in order to spare them pain. When no one talks about what's real, the youngest children fear they are hearing things and seeing things that may not even be happening. The kids also begin to believe they are the "crazy" ones. Such troubled youngsters are usually too embarrassed to turn to a school counselor, clergy person, relative, or friend for help. Instead they pretend—fantasizing about a loving, kind, caring, sane family. We have encountered adult children of alcoholics who suffered emotional and physical abuse and even incest and yet insisted that they came from a "normal" family. Children have a tremendous sense of loyalty to family, no matter what the cost. What a high price to pay. Kids who can't trust their parents lose trust in themselves and the security of their world. Without help, these children grow into adults unable to trust anyone.

Older Than Their Years

Children living in C.D. families take on responsibilities far too difficult for their years. Dedicated to family survival, they will do whatever is needed to keep the dysfunctional unit together. If children think the family needs someone to be perfect and take charge, they will. If they think it is necessary to take some focus off the chemically dependent person, they may act out and even get in trouble. If humor is needed, they will provide fun and games to the point of being obnoxious. Children will try to be perfect, serious, intellectual, or rebellious and troublesome, or even funny and cute—whatever works for right now. It is an exhausting job that makes young people quickly feel tired and scared, but they never stop trying. They fight paralyzing feelings of loneliness and guilt. There is no one to turn to, so the tears aren't shed and the screams aren't uttered.

Children get lost playing parts in the drama of the chemically dependent family. They lose touch with who is inside the pain, not allowing anyone—including themselves—to see, know, or love the person residing within the wall of defenses. It sometimes becomes necessary to withdraw or even become invisible to help the family. So some kids get harder and harder to find, suffocated beneath the weight of survival.

Where does childhood go for these children? It doesn't even exist. Adults who grew up in chemically dependent homes are typically intellectually overdeveloped and emotionally underdeveloped, often displaying compulsive behaviors like drinking, drugging, overeating, undereating, overworking, gambling, smoking, and indulging in promiscuous sex. They feel overtired, overworked, and overburdened and need help to deal with and grow out of their co-dependency. Without help, they will carry that pathology with them for as long as they live. Not only is their childhood taken away by this disease but, without help, healthy adulthood is impossible. It is critical to educate and intervene in the lives of young family members to stop this cruel cycle.

What's Family to a Child?

Kids in C.D. families believe that what is going on is "normal" unless someone tells them otherwise. We met an eleven-year-old whose dad would get drunk, get an ax, hold the child's head on a chopping block, and pretend he was going to cut off the boy's head. The youngster got so used to living this way that he thought being awakened in the middle of the night by a raging, drunken father and thrown against the wall was "normal." It is so important to reach these children and give them some idea of what a real family can be. Children living in a C.D. home also believe that the problems are their fault. Even the youngest must be told that they didn't cause chemical dependency and the living problems associated with this disease. A three-year-old girl once told us, "It's my fault that Daddy gets drunk." Then she would go stand in the corner and bite her arm until it bled. Even at this early age she was blaming herself.

Children must be told that they are not responsible. It is also important to break the no-talk rules in the family. When no one talks about what is real, people, particularly children, may not be able to distinguish reality. How does a child feel when he hears at school that love and moms and dads and pets and play are what families are all about and then goes home and sees drunkenness, physical fighting, and vomiting? And he listens to the screaming and the glass shattering in the night, trying to hide the fear by burying his face under the pillow and wondering what is real. What is family? What was family to the dark-eyed four-year-old girl at the Battered Women's Center who had lived through so much terror she couldn't talk to us, didn't react, didn't do anything—except sit and stare. What was family to the nine-year-old boy who thought he was the only one in his whole school living in a family like his? He felt so different and so scared. Relief shined in his eyes when he was told that many of his classmates lived in families just like his. He couldn't wait to join a group where he could talk to kids his own age who wouldn't think he was "crazy." Families?

Beware of Powerlessness

Family members try to stay in charge to survive. They pretend everything is going to be alright, developing a sense of powerlessness and resistance to change. The intolerable known becomes more acceptable than the frightening unknown. Family members seem to be saying to themselves, "Here at least I know my role, what I have to do to survive. Out there—who knows?" The fears seem insurmountable: where to go, what to do, who can help, where the money will come from. With trust gone, no one to talk to, and feelings buried, the idea of change—taking action and letting go of the chemically dependent person—is terrifying. They cling to the false security of the familiar. That is one of the reasons why adult children of alcoholics very often marry alcoholics—to repeat the role they have rehearsed. Often professionals hear co-dependent people describe their situation as intolerable. They can't continue and must do something. Yet after planning a course of action, they won't act, blocked by a wall of powerlessness. It is not easy to take back power and begin change. Staying stuck is much easier. It takes courage, trust, and action to recover, but the rewards are worth the risk.

A First Step

Recovery can begin by learning how to stop enabling. Those surrounding a chemically dependent person tend to do all the wrong things for all the right reasons: make excuses, pretend it's not so bad, lie, give the C.D. money, buy booze and drugs, bail the C.D. out of jail, and other rescue and cover-up operations. After a while, enabling becomes a difficult pattern to stop. Calling the boss and making excuses for the alcoholic gets easier. You believe that if you just get your child out of jail one more time, he will have learned his lesson and not drive drunk again. You learn just where to look for your husband's car after a night of drinking.

Enabling means accepting responsibility for the actions of the C.D., hoping that by doing all these helpful things you can stop him from drinking and drugging. But in fact, *by enabling, you are perpetuating the disease.* As long as the chemically dependent person pays little price for the drinking and drugging behavior, he has no reason to quit. Letting go of the reins is difficult. But when tempted to enable, remember you are literally loving him to death. By protecting the C.D. from the consequences of his unacceptable behavior, you deny him the opportunity to touch the true severity of the situation.

It is painful to let your husband lose his job, watch your child in jail, and listen to the abuse when you don't do what the C.D. person wants. It hurts to be reprimanded by well-meaning but ill-informed relatives and friends who think you should just care for him, love him, and pray for him until he recovers. Stop the enabling! Allow him the privilege of his pain! To do so, you will need the support of those who understand what you're going through, what works, and what doesn't work. Enabling is difficult if not impossible to stop without help. Feeling responsible and guilty will too easily lead back to enabling behaviors because they make you feel a little better about yourself, at least for a while.

Who Hits Bottom?

They speak of alcoholics "bottoming out." But what about family members hitting bottom? We usually think of family members as one day having enough and filing for divorce or insisting their C.D. adolescent accept treatment or disavowing their alcoholic parents or some other dramatic positive step. But this is not how co-dependent persons usually bottom out. Rather, it is more common to see them try to escape their pain through negative, self-defeating actions, which only aggravate their situation. For example, a wife may say, "I can't beat him, so I'll join him," and starts drinking abusively until she has her own drinking crisis. Or the child who simply cannot take any more turns to negative alternatives: drugs, dropping out, suicide. Tragically the family member may suffer as much trying to escape from the pain of co-dependency as the C.D.

experiences in the grips of chemical dependency. Who hits bottom? Everyone touched by this disease.

What Price Secrecy?

It's not easy to step outside of yourself and reach for help when your self-worth is constantly being bruised and battered. This blame-try-fail, blame-try-fail cycle wears away at self-esteem. Family members no longer feel confident enough to share the situation with others. They hide the pain—the physical illness, spiritual despair, terrible nightmares, shattered dreams, obsessions, compulsions, depressions, troubled relationships, failing grades, awful fears, isolation, the silent array of costly secrets. Ending this agony demands breaking this conspiracy of silence. And you'll need outside help to do it. A safe phone call is usually the easiest place to start.

Getting Started

Look in the yellow pages of your telephone directory under Alcoholism. Find Al-anon, Alateen, or Adult Children of Alcoholics support groups. If these groups are not listed, call Alcoholics Anonymous and ask about meetings for the families and friends of C.D. people. Request a call from Al-anon or Alateen.

   If you are a teenager, talk to your school counselor, nurse, or teacher about support groups within the school system. In such groups and in Alateen you will meet young people your age living in similar situations.

   Meetings for the adult children of alcoholics have sprung up all over the nation. The groups are called ACOA or ACA Al-anon groups. Another organization, Co-dependency Anonymous, is found in some communities. These various support groups can save your life. They are not meant to be therapy groups, but they do provide a source of experience, strength, and hope.

   It is important to find a place where you can express your true feelings and where it's safe to talk about them. Listen closely. The people who are sharing may express a feeling that you yourself have been afraid to voice. Hold on to them for support until able to express your own. Newcomers are welcome and very special. Check it out. Discover you're not alone! Seek out a more experienced member, someone you can trust who will keep you in touch with reality and help you escape the vicious cycle. This person, called a sponsor, will be someone to talk with, contact in crisis, and assist you in launching your recovery. Find someone who really cares about you. When your family is no longer there for you emotionally, it is crucial to find a substitute place where it's safe to talk and feel.

Just How Serious Is This?

Co-dependency, without help, is a lifelong permanent condition affecting the victim in all subsequent relationships. Untreated co-dependents pass on delusion, repression, and compulsion to their own children. Recovery requires therapy or treatment. You cannot simply learn or think your way out of co-dependency because it is burned into your heart and soul.

An eighteen-year-old high school senior, tears running down his cheeks, approached us after a presentation. He told us that he never knew that the behavior of his alcoholic parents could have a lifelong affect on him. Now he understood why he was like he was and wanted help to change. He was weary from his struggle to survive the chaos of an alcoholic home.

A Special Word to Parents

Parents of chemically dependent offspring also take on enabling roles and survival behaviors. So most of what has been said concerning spouses and children in co-dependency applies to parents as well. However, the major trap for most parents is that they give up their authority. They allow the troubled child to take charge of the family, control its emotional life, and drive its behavior.

Parents must regain their rightful power. Mothers and fathers of children with alcohol or drug problems should first learn the laws of their state concerning compulsory treatment. It may be that they can require their son or daughter to enter an appropriate recovery program. Above all, parents need to set limits and stick to them. This may even require involving law enforcement officials. More than one C.D. adolescent has gone from a judge's chambers to a treatment center. To demonstrate such tough love, parents will need the help of a support group, such as Toughlove Parents or Al-anon. Co-dependency is multigenerational and moves in all directions. You can get it from your kids.

A Road Now Well-Traveled

Fortunately, excellent individual co-dependency treatment and family-based chemical dependency treatment are now available. Support groups as well as co-dependency-focused therapy groups are available in nearly every community. Keep in mind there is no blame in either chemical dependency or co-dependency. These are diseases that nobody asked for and everyone got. But it is no longer necessary to just survive. The right kind of help can free your real feelings from the depths of your pain and restore your authentic self. Family members who have cried and screamed their way through layers of hurt and pain come out the other side knowing that, deep down, they are real. Real, feeling human being.

3

Hazards on the Way to Help

Caution: The Usual Help...May Not!

Finding the excellent care now available for chemical dependency and co-dependency poses special challenges. The inclination is for suffering families to turn to the mainstream helping professions: physicians, psychologists, clergy persons, marriage counselors, social workers. After all, that is where our experience teaches us to go for "professional help." Yet, for alcohol and other drug-related problems, such resources must be carefully screened.

As late as the early 1980s, very few schools of medicine, ministry, psychology, or social work offered in-depth courses in alcoholism or other chemical dependencies. The general theme in the health care professions reflected society's view that alcohol and drug abuse were behavioral or criminal justice problems. Consequently, most physicians, clergy, psychologists, and social workers were not trained to deal with these issues as primary illnesses. C.D. was seen as secondary to some underlying moral, behavioral, or psychological problem.

How Bad Is It?

He'd recently been fired from a bank presidency. His once significant net worth was in virtual collapse. Now he was sitting across from us weeping. "Why didn't anybody tell me these things before?" he asked through the tears. Let's call him John. John had told us a story we'd heard many times before. Job stress drove him to his doctor, who prescribed a tranquilizer and continued to do so for years. Several physicians, jobs, and cross-country "geographical cure" moves later, his life was in shambles—all because of the pills. He was experiencing panic attacks, chronic anxiety, bouts of paranoia, every area of his life was falling apart. Another psychiatrist prescribed a different tranquilizer. Then a psychologist referred him to a third doctor, whose solution was more pills. None of the physicians, psychiatrists, or psychologists involved in his case for over ten years ever questioned his use of or need for tranquilizers. In a real sense, they were his pushers.

The banker entered C.D. treatment and—glory be!—a miracle. His stress, panic attacks, anxiety, paranoia, and eventually his professional and financial problems faded from his now sober and productive life. The banker's wife and teenage children, who had been severely affected by this chaos, also underwent treatment. They are a normal happy family again.

Beware the Professional Enabler

It is fair to say that many helping professionals have entered the business of treating chemically dependent and co-dependent people without the proper education and training. In the 1970s and 80s, many physicians, counselors and therapists of other disciplines opened treatment centers and clinics or offered therapy groups in response to increased public awareness and demand for treatment. Most of these health professionals made the effort to gain the prerequisite skills needed to offer excellent programs. But a few were simply incompetent and/or dollar-driven, with their facilities staffed with profit rather than professional competency in mind. One could witness the inappropriate prescribing of tranquilizers to already chemically dependent persons, the charging of high fees for ineffective talk therapy, ACOA groups conducted by counselors who should have been in one...and the list could go on.

In recent years the system has purged itself of much of this abuse. But the unwary can still blunder into what is called professional enabling. So a warning is in order. There are at least seven ways untrained, unhealthy, or ill-intended helping professionals can enable a C.D. person to continue in self-destructive ways.

1. Not recognizing and diagnosing the primary problem as chemical dependency or co-dependency.

2. Not confronting the patient about drinking/drugging.

3. Prescribing or dispensing mood-altering chemicals.

4. Failing to refer patients to specialized treatment and, instead, employing inappropriate forms of psychotherapy.

5. Rescuing, judging, problem-solving, or avoiding the real issues, thus provoking even deeper feelings of powerlessness, inadequacy, guilt, and isolation in the chemically dependent person and/or family.

6. Suggesting ineffective courses of action based on lack of information or misinformation.

7. Being actively chemically dependent themselves.

Where to Turn

Until recently there were few formal courses in alcohol or other drug dependencies. It is only in the last five years or so that degree programs have emerged. Consequently, most of the professionals competent in the C.D. field achieved their knowledge and skill through continuing education programs and specialized internships rather than in their initial professional education and training. Consequently, top-notch C.D. specialists are quite knowledgeable, intensely dedicated, and very capable, but not always easy to find. They are now beginning to surface in mainstream health care. One reason is that, until the mid 1970s, there was little insurance coverage for treatment of alcoholism and other chemical dependencies. Consequently, with little economic incentive, few conventional hospitals or psychiatric facilities were interested in providing care to "drunks, dope fiends, or their crazy friends and relatives," especially since these patients denied they had a problem, resented attempts to be helped, were often belligerent, and sometimes even smelled bad. To fill these voids, a network of paraprofessional counselors and freestanding nonhospital treatment facilities evolved during the fifties, sixties, and seventies. However, a combination of government funding, expanded insurance coverage, and growing public enlightenment led to new involvement on the part of the orthodox helping professions and institutions.

The paraprofessionals and free-standing programs deserve credit for developing the early treatment models. But it must be acknowledged that the conventional helping professionals and health care institutions have the credentialing networks and financial wherewithal needed to mass-produce this help for the many millions in need.

The best of both worlds was emerging in the eighties and nineties. The proven programs and skills developed by the dedicated pioneers were adopted by the national health care organizations that, with their business acumen and financial strength, could deliver them on a large scale. At present, however, the intervention and treatment of alcohol and other drug dependencies is still in a state of transition. The concept of "managed care," which one critic described as "neither," has emerged. Originally, a positive step to curtail rising health care costs, managed care has evolved into an antagonistic dialogue between insurance providers and care givers.

This growing negative component in our national health care system is much too complex to deal with here. Until this jockeying for position settles down, finding affordable, effective help for your situation may require some effort in order to avoid help that doesn't help. (See Chapters 12 and 13 for help in finding quality resources.)

So for Now, Be Careful

Our clients have revealed how a naive walk through the Yellow Pages looking for help wound up costing time, money, and emotional pain with no results. There are many variations, but the essence of the tale usually goes as follows. It seems they had first sought help where conditioned to seek it: psychiatrists, clergy persons, physicians, marriage counselors, psychologists, school counselors, and social workers. Yet often the information received was outdated or inaccurate and the advice inappropriate. Worst of all, expensive, unnecessary, and even harmful medication or therapy was often prescribed. The message is this: if care is not taken, you may encounter professionals who can delay, block, and even do harm to recovery while charging a lot of money. These perhaps well-intended "professional enablers" in one way or another permit suffering families to continue on destructive courses of action. Consider the following real-life examples.

Case Study—"The Woman Who Had Everything"

Not only did Ruth have everything, but it seemed she was taking everything there was for it. Ruth first got into "help" when she showed up in the hospital emergency room with an apparent allergic reaction. The emergency staff failed to note that Ruth's eyes were bloodshot, speech slurred, gait very unsteady, and breath nearly flammable. The doctor prescribed a shot and referred her to an allergist. He suggested an isolation diet, which she carefully followed. But she continued drinking her bourbon because the doctor never mentioned that.

A few days later another reaction sent her back to the emergency room. Her puzzled allergist ran a comprehensive series of skin and blood tests, and prescribed twice-weekly desensitization shots and powerful antihistamines. Still no questions about her alcohol use. Ruth paid little attention to the warnings about mixing the pills with alcohol because she "didn't drink that much." She found herself awakening drowsy from the pills and discovered that a Bloody Mary got her moving.

Later, while seeing her doctor for a sore throat, she reported extreme nervousness. He prescribed "a tranquilizer to tide her over the rough spots." Still no discussion of alcohol use except a reminder not to drink while taking the tranquilizer. Ruth interpreted this as meaning "Don't wash it down with a beer." By this time her alcoholism had progressed to the point where her blood pressure was elevated and required drugs to control. Her doctor also detected mild diabetes and added medication for that condition as well. He did caution her to restrict her drinking, but there was no real discussion of alcohol as a possible factor in her growing array of physical problems.

As Ruth's alcoholism progressed, she developed gastrointestinal problems that led to many examinations, x-rays, and medications but no clear diagnosis. Finally, her various physicians began refusing to renew her tranquilizer prescription. One eventually referred her to a psychiatrist. After reviewing her medical epoch, he prescribed antidepressant drugs. By now Ruth was suffering from allergies, sleep disorders, nervousness, headaches, gastrointestinal distress, diabetes, high blood pressure, and depression—for all of which she was taking some kind of medication. And like most chemically dependent people, she was further assaulting her body and central nervous system with huge doses of nicotine and caffeine.

Ruth's family attended a community information program we presented. Coming up to us afterwards, her husband described all the maladies from which she was suffering and exclaimed, "We hate to say anything about her drinking because she's so sick all the time. Her bourbon is all she has to look forward to." After education, training, and counseling they successfully intervened and entered family treatment. The medical director, a specialist in C.D., weaned her from all medications within a week. Miraculously, her allergies, high blood pressure, nervousness, sleep problems, gastrointestinal distress, depression, and diabetes disappeared as she recovered from her primary disease—alcoholism.

Is this an isolated or far-fetched example? Ask the medical director of any good C.D. treatment center. He or she could keep you up nights relating countless similar medical melodramas. The reality is that most physicians and psychiatrists are neither trained to recognize or motivated to confront anything but very late, near-fatal symptoms of alcoholism: cirrhosis, acute pancreatitus, delirium tremens, and specific kinds of skin disease and muscle weakness. Short of that, they will, as in Ruth's case, usually just diagnose and treat symptoms. Like many of us, physicians are reluctant to question patients about alcohol use either because they consider it a personal matter, because there is an implied stigma, or because it brings into question their own alcohol or drug use.

Lesson: Alcoholism, when present in an ill person, is almost always the primary chronic disease. Except for emergency treatment of acute injuries, internal bleeding, or overdoses, it is futile to treat C.D. persons for other diseases until they first undergo treatment of their primary illness.

Case Study—"The Battered Christian"

Sarah approached us cautiously after one of our information programs. Her bruised arms and face bore witness to recent violence. After some evasion and many furtive glances, Sarah admitted that her alcoholic spouse beat her severely on frequent occasions. Her reason for not leaving or at least seeking help was her minister's counsel that her husband was just a sinful man who needed to repent. He insisted it was her Christian duty to remain with him and that all she could do to help was pray. The preacher suggested that Jesus would want her to turn the other cheek.

In all our programs we urge people living in physical abuse situations to seek help through local shelters for battered women, law enforcement agencies, or appropriate social service organizations. The first priority should be their own life and limb. And they certainly can't earn a living, care for children, or help the chemically dependent person if paralyzed with fear, physically incapacitated, or dead.

After some urging, the terrified woman sought safety and counseling at the Battered Women's Center. We also referred her to a minister of her faith who had more current and enlightened education about chemical dependency and family violence. With his support, her husband was confronted about the abuse and offered treatment for his alcoholism and associated violent behavior. Grudgingly he agreed, only because she refused to come home if he did not.

This points out an exciting reality of modern C.D. treatment today: quality treatment is effective even when the C.D. person enters a program under coercion and filled with anger. And so it was in this case. During his treatment for alcoholism, the husband learned that his abusive behavior was related not only to his alcohol use, but also to his upbringing in a family where his own father had been an abusive alcoholic. He learned how someone raised in this kind of emotionally deprived family develops a disturbed emotional life and an array of self-defeating survival behaviors. Consequently. the husband had to deal with the emotional and behavioral impacts of not only his own alcoholism but also his family's.

After a period of sobriety, the husband joined an ACOA therapy group. Here he was able to purge his repressed childhood anger and to deal with frustration without resorting to physical violence. The family is now living and growing together in peace.

Lesson: Clergy are not necessarily trained C.D. counselors. If there is a need for pastoral counseling, contact the local council of churches or the seminary that educates the ministers of your church. They can probably steer you to someone qualified.

Case Study—"The Medicated Family"

Kathy, the oldest daughter, spoke to us after a program we presented at her college. Through slowed and halting speech, Kathy told us she was having trouble with her schoolwork and was under the care of a physician who had prescribed antidepressants. She sensed that somehow her problems were related to her father's alcoholism. After some encouragement, Kathy brought her mother to our next information session. The mother confirmed her husband's alcohol problem and added that he also took sleeping pills and tranquilizers. Prescribed by the same doctor who was treating the daughter, this mixture was supposed "to help him deal with his job stress and cut down on his drinking." Further discussion uncovered that Mom was using large amounts of tranquilizers daily prescribed by—you guessed it—the same doctor "to help her cope during this trying time." And Debbie, another daughter, was taking medication for her hyperactivity, also dispensed by the family doctor. To round out the chemical scene, their teenage son, we learned, was a heavy marijuana smoker. So here was an entire family under the influence of some kind of mood-altering chemical. And all this drug use, except the son's, was courtesy of the well-intended family physician.

After much counseling, a successful intervention on Dad's alcoholism led to treatment. During Family Week at the treatment center, the chemical use by the rest of the family was revealed. After outpatient treatment for all of them and a considerable period of aftercare, the entire family was chemical-free. A sober Dad, equipped with a clear head and putting in a full day's work, found that most of his "job stress" had been generated by alcoholism. Mom accepted her powerlessness over tranquilizers just as her husband had alcohol. She learned how to deal with her feelings openly and honestly, to assert her needs before she became angry and frustrated, and to feel good about herself. She joined a self-help group with a program for living that led to new, positive, and supportive friends. Down the drain went her remaining tranquilizers. Kathy, whose courage in reaching out for help no doubt saved the family, was taken off medication by the knowledgeable physician at the treatment center who suspected that her depression was not primary, but the result of living in an alcoholic family.

Frequently the depression seen in chemically dependent family members is simply anger turned inward because it's not safe to express it openly. In this case, after Kathy was able to process her anger in the safety of family treatment, her depression and the need for medication disappeared. Likewise, Debbie's hyperactivity quickly faded once peace returned to the family. And so too her need for medication. Junior's marijuana abuse was confronted in family treatment and, after learning that his grandfather and great grandfather had both been alcoholic, he wisely chose to abstain.

Unsnarling drug-controlled families like this isn't easy. A family, presenting a complex array of problems such as depression, job stress, marriage conflicts, hyperactivity, and teenage rebellion, usually requires specialists to diagnose this underlying primary disease.

Lesson: If you suspect alcohol or drugs are a problem in a family member, find out whether your doctor has special training in C.D. If not, get the name of one who does from a local treatment center.

Case Study—"Super Drunk"

Like most C.D. people, Walter's disease began to disrupt all areas of his life—professional, family, health, spiritual, and financial. And like many other C.D. victims, he tried to fix each of these in turn with counseling, enlightenment, self-improvement programs, and greater effort. In his own words, "First my wife and I went to marriage counseling because she thought that one of the reasons for my drinking and pot-smoking was communication problems. In counseling I learned to express my needs more honestly, give feedback, listen actively, and empathize with Shirley's feelings.

At the counselor's suggestion, Shirley attended assertiveness training and I went to a stress management course. After that, whenever Shirley would very assertively confront my drinking, I would listen attentively with glass in hand, accurately feed back what she had said, empathize with her concern, and acknowledge that she deserved a sober mate. Then, I'd take another drink to calm my nerves. Later, I got into yoga, and if things got too hot and heavy, I'd ask for some space and go meditate." Walter went to night school for two different work-related graduate degrees. And, as part of this "higher" education, mastered the use of uppers and downers to orchestrate his study habits. He also got into cocaine as a "recreational drug" by way of a relationship with a female fellow student who "understood him" better than his wife. She understood him well enough to bring on a divorce, which left him so broke that she quickly stopped understanding him. All this time he was on a fast track at the company after a series of rapid and important promotions. Then came the crash. Walter made the papers with a D.W.I. So, when Walter began to make mistakes at work, the company was already primed to intervene and insist he accept help.

Underneath all his apparent success, Walter's drinking and drugging had created three very dysfunctional families; he was beginning to show signs of liver disease; and, while under the influence of drugs, he had made some very questionable business deals. All of this, plus fear of losing his job, made Walter despondent. As he said, "The headline was about to read 'Young Businessman's Success Story Ends in Shocking Suicide.'"

Walter's story is not uncommon. Many C.D. people cover up their disease with overachievement on and off the job. Walter tried to overcome his loss of control over alcohol by demonstrating that he was too smart and capable to get hooked on alcohol and drugs. He tried to conquer the unacceptable conduct, emotional pain, and defensive behavior by proving over and over that he was sane, intelligent, successful, and physically fit. This piecemeal approach to conquering C.D. is like attending to pest control when the house is on fire.

Lesson: Just as C.D. is the primary disease and must be treated first, so too it is the primary life problem and must be dealt with before attempting to overcome whatever other problems it may have caused.

Far Too Many

Helping professionals can be constrained by the threat of stigmatizing their patients, limited by poor training, and confused by the myths that still surround C.D. These deficiencies can affect the way they interact with chemically dependent people and their families. And many of these professionals may themselves be suffering from co-dependency. Whatever the reason, their ineptness can actually worsen the condition. These are not isolated cases. This "harmful help" is still evident in many communities. Even in today's more enlightened times, many practicing physicians, psychiatrists, psychologists, clergy, and social workers have received little current education in the intervention and treatment of C.D. There are notable exceptions, but it is true that most of the schools they attended devoted only a few hours of curriculum to what many feel is the nation's number one health problem. University schools of psychology and social work are still teaching future therapists that alcoholism and other chemical dependencies are symptoms of underlying psychological or emotional disorders. And at the many workshops we've conducted for the clergy of numerous denominations, priests and ministers report little or no training in what, after a few years in a position, they consider to be the major problem in their congregations.

Shining Examples

On the other hand, we fondly remember a clergyman very dear to us who encountered a family he couldn't help because he knew so little about alcoholism. Recognizing this need in his ministry, he went back to school for a year to study C.D. We also know a young psychiatrist who admitted his ignorance about chemical problems and, with an open mind, set about becoming a nationally respected medical expert on chemical dependency.

We are aware of many respected professionals who give of their time and talents to those unable to pay. There are such quiet heroes in the professional ranks. We've also encountered physicians who gave up time from their practices to present their medical opinions in family intervention sessions. Their presence had a powerful impact on the outcome. Finally, we especially applaud those courageous physicians, clergy, and other helping professionals who have publicly announced their own recovery from chemical dependency. In some cases these disclosures jeopardized their positions but seemed worth the price in order to help end the suffering of others.

C.D. Is a Speciality

There are many such horror stories in our experience, but perhaps this is enough evidence to make the point: proceed with hope but be careful. Clearly the intervention and treatment of chemical dependency and co-dependency requires special education, training, and skills as well as a high level of personal growth on the part of the professionals involved. It is, therefore, important to seek out healthy, properly trained, and effective help resources. As with any other disease, look for the highly regarded specialist with a record of success. Qualified physicians can be identified by their certification from the American Society of Addiction Medicine.

Addictionology is now an identified medical speciality with 3,500 members nationally. Check with your county medical society for the names of local physicians who have this special training and background. The National Association of Alcoholism and Drug Abuse Counselors has 15,000 members. This organization has set rigid and high standards for certification in this challenging health specialty. Thus, there is a high-quality, affordable, effective care available for the intervention and treatment of chemical dependency and co-dependency. These professional resources are set firmly atop a national network of specialty help programs such as A.A., Al-anon, Alateen, Adult Children of Alcoholics, Narcotics Anonymous, Tough Love Parents, Cocaine Anonymous, and many others.

Follow the proven paths. Join an appropriate support group. This network of new friends and acquaintances can help in recommending and checking out potential therapists, intervention counselors, and treatment programs. And remember, the resources you choose should work for you. Tell them the truth and cooperate with them. But if things don't change, move on—examine other options. Find a person or program that works.

Part Two

Taking Action

4

Six Critical Actions

What Does It Take?

There are direct, dollar-wise paths to reversing the course of C.D. and its family impact. Quality, affordable help is out there for the asking. Still, the situation can seem overwhelming—a bit like opening your child's new bicycle box on Christmas Eve, seeing all those loose parts and complicated directions, and realizing the project should have been started a long time ago. Yet carefully following the tested directions can produce a gift that brings years of joy. That's also what it takes for family recovery. Following tested directions works. Just face each piece of the task one at a time and heed proven guidelines; the end product will be the gift of lifetime wellness for you and your loved ones.

The way is now quite clearly defined by those who have gone before you. Helpful choices and positive actions—based on accurate information, professional guidance, and clearly defined goals—can reverse the damage that has been done and lead to full recovery.

There Is a High Road

The ideal scenario is timely intervention followed by quality treatment leading to lifetime recovery. Not just for the C.D. person but for all those impacted by the disease. Such a level of restoration may seem an abstract idea or an imagined wonderland. Yet if you take the right actions, you will eventually cross the magic line beyond which you are no longer a suffering person seeking wellness but a well person growing toward your highest potential. You'll wake up one day and recognize that your personal world has become a far more open, honest, congruent place. A more positive environment, where healthy loved ones relate as equals and from which the unhealthy have been denied citizenship. An atmosphere in which honest feelings are now respected and individuality is possible. As distant and elusive as all that may sound, such a level of wellness is entirely possible within the present state of the intervention and treatment art. Getting there is a matter of wanting it bad enough to do what it takes. Recovery requires willingness, risk, effort, and, most of all, new and better choices leading to critical actions.

Recovery Planning

Like any complex human endeavor, recovery from this family illness will demand time, money, energy, and motivation. So it is wise to plan carefully. With a bit of forethought you'll get there faster, spend less money, and achieve higher levels of wellness for you and your family. Recovery is simply undoing what C.D. did. It is a move-by-move strategy to deal one by one with the components of the disease. This takes a willingness to be open to new ideas and normally requires the help of trained professionals.

In this chapter, the focus will be on the Six Critical Actions we usually observe in those who have successfully reversed the damage done to them and their families by alcohol or other drugs. These choices are a logical sequence to recovery, attacking the disease in much the same sequence as it unfolded.

Six Critical Actions

The following is a checklist of the sequential components of recovery:

1. Seek accurate, current information.

2. Arrange a professional assessment.

3. Join a support group.

4. Learn intervention skills.

5. Pursue the goal of family-based treatment.

6. Follow through after treatment.

The following is a description of each Critical Action and suggestions on how to carry it out. These actions can be postponed or dragged out for years, or they can all be commenced in the course of a single day. But sooner or later most people find them critical to the pursuit of quality recovery.

1. Seek Accurate, Current Information

A nonthreatening and easy-to-take first move is to seek out books, articles, films, and community education programs that provide up-to-date information about how alcohol and other drugs affect individuals and families. The first stop on the road to recovery ought to be the library or book store. Book therapy can be invaluable because it is helpful, inexpensive, and nonthreatening. And books only charge for the first visit.

There is a short list of recommended reading in the back of this book. Our clients have consistently found these titles helpful. All of the authors listed have achieved national recognition for breakthroughs in understanding and treating chemical dependency and co-dependency.

As you examine potential reading material, keep in mind that these diseases primarily reside at the feeling level. Be suspect of heady intellectual books. Leave these scholarly works with the psycho-babble titles to the expert in search of greater expertise. In-depth information can come later. For now, intervention and initial recovery requires but few facts and much action. The hurt cannot be understood or intellectualized away. It must be owned, experienced, and converted to positive energies. These are not diseases that require a lot of clinical language to explain. The word *powerlessness* has more clarity than *compulsivity*, and *unloved* is easier to understand than *emotional deprivation*. Certainly, the specificity of clinical verbiage has a place in the training of professionals, but in early recovery it's best to keep it simple. The goal is not to get smarter but to feel better and live life more fully.

Community Information Programs

Reading will probably increase your desire to know more about how alcohol and drugs affect families. Workshops, seminars, and other community information programs have advantages over simply reading about these problems. Such gatherings remove some of the sense of isolation, allow you to ask questions, and assist in identifying help resources.

Hospitals and other treatment facilities recognize the community relations value derived from sponsoring free community information lectures or seminars about alcohol, drugs, and family intervention. Consequently, professionally conducted introductory presentations are likely to be available at little or no cost. Call the local Council on Alcoholism for the schedule. The council, which is listed in the Yellow Pages under "Alcoholism Information" (the term "drug abuse" may also be in the title), is a United Way agency found in nearly every major community. If receiving mail from the council will not cause problems for you, it's a helpful idea to get your name on the mailing list for its very informative newsletters.

Do They Know What They're Talking About?

Once the various information programs available in your town are identified, there are ways to check out their quality. Call the sponsoring agency and ask: Who presents the program? What is it about? How long has the program been offered? How large is the usual attendance? Is it open to the general public? There are no right or wrong answers to these questions. Any program presented by a reputable treatment organization will likely be helpful. What is important, however, is how your questions are answered. If the community information program is professionally done, well organized, and successful in attracting large and diverse audiences, it will be a source of pride to the organization. Listen for professionalism as your questions are answered. Be wary if the call is passed to several persons or no one seems to know about the program. Or if responsibility for the program is rotated through several staff members or the schedule of presentation dates and times is not readily available. All these are signs that the program doesn't have much priority in the organization and is probably not of high quality.

2. Arrange a Professional Assessment

Once you have a clearer understanding of what is happening, it is time to meet with a professional alcohol and drug abuse counselor to discuss your situation and sort things out. He or she can help develop an overall intervention and treatment plan for your family. But finding the right person for the job is not easy. Here are some precepts to keep in mind when selecting a counselor or other helping professional:

- Alcohol and drug abuse counselors, psychologists, and other professional helpers are fundamentally service providers—they work for you. They should honor their appointment times, answer your questions satisfactorily, empathize with your feelings, and provide real help for your problems. On the other hand, counselors have a right to respect, to full and truthful information, to cooperation with recommended treatment, to on-time arrivals for appointments, and to timely payment for services rendered.

- It's O.K. to fire incompetent help. If the professional person to whom you have turned for assistance doesn't respond to your needs—terminate. But keep in mind that, although your feelings deserve empathy and questions should be answered satisfactorily, you may not always like the professional who is trying to help you. Often the counselor may have to get tough, be confrontive, suggest scary risks, or even terminate the therapy in your own best interests. But through all of that, you as a client should feel important, respected, and—most of all—that you're being helped. If nothing is changing, you have a perfect right to seek out someone else.

- Check out the professional with the community. Helping professionals quickly get a reputation—good or bad. Ask around at self-help meetings. Talk to friends you trust. Ask other professionals. Nurses are a valuable source of information about physicians. Clergy can often recommend ethical therapists. The local Council on Alcoholism can suggest alcohol and drug abuse counselors, intervention consultants, and treatment programs. A bit of effort will find competent people with the right skills and solid professional reputations.

3. Join a Support Group

Getting involved in Al-anon, Alateen, Adult Children of Alcoholics, Tough Love Parents, or a similar group is vital. You just can't do all this alone. If you could, you would have done so a long time ago. Now that you are making these better choices, you'll need a positive program for living in this negative situation and a source of emotional support for taking the remaining actions.

Self-help programs, especially those based on the famous Twelve Steps of A.A., can be of most value if viewed as one part of the total framework of recovery. First of all, self-help programs, as important as they are to recovery, do not fully meet the needs of everyone. A.A., for example, has met relatively little success among minorities, especially black communities. Neither A.A. nor its sister programs Al-anon and Alateen for family members fully address all the issues now identified as critical to family recovery. For example, many female children from C.D. families have experienced sexual abuse. Self-help programs are not structured to offer the safe, professionally facilitated, therapeutic environment in which such powerful trauma can be healed. Thus, getting into a support group is crucial to recovery, but it is not the total answer.

4. Learn Intervention Skills

Often just taking the three Critical Actions described above will cause the C.D. person to accept help. When the disease is better understood, professional guidance is obtained, and the enabling stops, the C.D. person suddenly finds that his previous behavior is no longer being tolerated while help options are being presented in a more acceptable format. This combination of circumstances may serve to intervene.

But if the C.D. person is still in denial, you may want to learn more powerful ways to intervene. Your counselor can teach you how to use crisis as a focal point for intervention attempts. He or she can also refine your communications skills for use during the one-on-one intervention attempts that arise so often when living or working with an active C.D. person.

The counselor may advise a series of meetings at which the significant people in the C.D. person's life receive the general education, specific training, individual coaching, and co-dependency counseling necessary to prepare for a formal intervention attempt. These sessions may culminate in a gathering at which examples of the C.D. person's unacceptable alcohol- or other drug-related behavior are presented. The meeting is conducted in a nonjudgmental fashion and in an atmosphere of concern. The C.D. person is also told of the emotional impact his drinking and/or drugging has had on those who care. Help is then offered that he can accept with dignity.

An intervention planning meeting between yourself, a trained intervention counselor, and perhaps one or two of the other persons concerned about the C.D.'s problem can be very beneficial. With their input you can intelligently explore the potential for a formal intervention attempt upon the C.D. person. If such an effort seems appropriate, the counselor will help put together a detailed intervention plan. (See Chapter 8 for more details about intervention.)

5. Pursue the Goal of Family-Based Treatment

By now the actions taken should produce the courage and motivation to begin the search for treatment. Phone calls, visits, and other inquiries are necessary in order to find the right resource for your family's situation.

What Is Treatment?

The treatment of alcoholism and other drug dependencies today is the culmination of several decades of experiment, trial and error, and feedback from those treated. Programs today combine the best of psychotherapy, the twelve-step self-help programs, medicine, nutrition, and fitness plus an eclectic milieu of peripheral approaches such as relaxation training, assertiveness skills, occupational therapy, and so forth.

Treatment centers are like any other service. To be successful they must develop and maintain a core of satisfied "customers" speaking well of them in the community. In this case the satisfied "customers" are in the form of sober, happy, productive recovered alcoholics and other types of C.D. people. Treatment today is a big, highly competitive business. Thus, to keep and expand market share, these programs must work well now and keep getting better.

How Good Are Treatment Programs?

A reasonable and conservative estimate of the C.D. persons who enter a respected treatment program and achieve and maintain lifetime sobriety would be in the range of 50 percent to 60 percent. Keep in mind, however, that many others who relapse quickly recover and then stay sober for life. Hardly anybody ever undergoes treatment and reverts right back to his or her old ways. "If nothing else, it ruins their drinking" is often quipped.

When the family of a relapsing C.D. person has undergone treatment, learned to stop enabling, and is pursuing their own recovery, the C.D. person quickly realizes that no one will tolerate unacceptable behavior any longer.

There is no central source of data on the pros and cons or the successes and failures of various treatment approaches. Limited availability of official report cards notwithstanding, there are widely held beliefs about which treatment methods and practices work and which do not. In the absence of hard data, economics is often a useful way to wring out the truth of things. So, in seeking to define effective treatment, it is useful to look at the kind of treatment for which business and industry is willing to pay. Most companies of any size have come to realize that untreated C.D. is a major cause of attendance, performance, and behavior problems on the job. There are estimates as high as a hundred billion dollars a year in lost workplace productivity. Consequently, just about every large business and many small ones have established employee assistance programs through which to intervene and help C.D. employees. Such EAPs, as these help programs are called, continuously check out the treatment centers to which they refer C.D. employees and follow up on the results achieved. In this way companies review the way their health care monies are spent in an effort to control cost. So when deciding on a treatment program it may be a good idea to follow the lead of the employee assistance professionals.

Treatment Selection Guidelines

The following criteria, used by employee assistance program managers to identify quality treatment, may be of value in your quest:

- *Select the lowest-cost care commensurate with the needs of the client.* C.D. is the only illness in which it is customary to focus the best resources and highest cost care on those with the earliest stages of the disease. Conversely, as a victim experiences serious relapses and enters the later terminal stages, ever-cheaper, lower-quality, and less effective treatment is employed. Then when they get chronically devastated, it is customary to abandon them to die in the streets or under a bridge somewhere. In other words, the quality and duration of treatment is often determined by the insurance benefits available and not the clinical needs of the patient. This is like putting someone with high blood pressure and dangerous cholesterol levels in the intensive coronary care unit, then later—when he has a heart attack—sending him to a neighborhood clinic, and finally—when heart failure takes place—letting him die in the streets or perhaps in a jail cell.

Recommendation: If the C.D. person still has a primary career, a job, a family, and reasonable physical health, it is sensible to look into the relatively inexpensive and very effective outpatient programs now being offered. Or, if the professionals with whom you are working believe that inpatient care is advisable, ask them to consider a combination of inpatient/outpatient. However, in opting for these more economical programs, be sure the family component offered is intensive enough to meet the needs of the entire family.

- *Match treatment to socioeconomic status and special needs.* Years ago it was a common practice to treat C.D. people of all backgrounds and ages in the same programs, the idea being that they shared a common problem that responded to a universal solution. Experience has shown this to be an unwise approach. Adolescents, street-drug users, women, single women with young children, older citizens, gay persons, minorities, and certain professions such as clergy, physicians, and many other definable groups respond better to treatment programs built to meet their special needs.

Recommendation: Attend open A.A., Al-anon, or other support group meetings such as ACOA gatherings. Talk to people to whom you feel the C.D. person would relate and ask them for suggestions about treatment facilities. Then call, write, or visit these facilities and talk to a staff member. See enough and hear enough to decide whether the facility feels right for your family. Remember, like EAP managers, you're paying for services and have every right to shop.

- *Use only those programs with well-developed and proven family-oriented inpatient or outpatient treatment for those family and other concerned persons identified by the treatment staff as co-dependent.* These programs combine education with individual and group therapies. Heavy emphasis is placed on group therapy in which painful feelings can be processed. Some of the therapy may involve the C.D. person.

Recommendation: Arrange to speak to the director of the family treatment component. Describe your situation and feelings and ask what the program will do for you and other family members. See if the answer is responsive to your needs. You may not hear what you want to hear but what you need to hear. Listen less to your head than to your heart.

- *Be certain that the program includes a professionally directed, therapeutic aftercare component.* EAP managers place strong emphasis on the contribution to long-term recovery that results from professionally conducted aftercare.

Recommendation: Select a treatment program that insists on specific aftercare commitments from its graduating patients and aids them in connecting with the community-based resources needed to sustain recovery.

Measuring Success

On the surface it would seem that the proper measuring stick to rate various treatment centers would be to compare track records. The problem is that there are so many tracks. Furthermore, since most treatment outcome studies are prepared by the treatment facilities themselves, the numbers are difficult to validate. Nor is there even agreed-upon criteria for determining treatment success. Is it continued abstinence two years after treatment? Maybe. One ex-patient may have a relapse six months after treatment, which leads to real acceptance of his disease, and then may pursue sobriety and personal growth with great progress. Another may refuse to follow his aftercare commitments, fail to attend A.A., and generally be miserable to be around—but somehow manage not to drink. Which of the two should be counted as a success? Seemingly, abstinence alone is probably an inadequate indicator of the quality of recovery. Or a treatment program may boast of a high "still-sober-after-two-years" rate but have such a weak family program that the only one who is really getting well is the C.D. person. Surely that is not a quality program.

Another flaw in comparing recovery rates between treatment programs is that some may only count the patients who *completed* their program. The dropouts literally drop out of the statistics. Such a program may boast an 80 percent recovery rate without stating that perhaps half of its patients never complete the full treatment regimen.

To further complicate the situation, a truly excellent facility may sometimes therapeutically discharge uncooperative patients because their presence is contaminating the treatment of others. But if this facility measures its success rate against the number of patients who initially enter the program, it may compare poorly with a facility that only counted "graduates." Yet this facility may well have a program of greater integrity and be of more value to the patients who actually complete its program.

Trust Your Gut and the Wisdom of the Marketplace

Valid treatment outcome studies require expertise in double-blind studies and multivariate statistical analysis. Such skills are not readily available in C.D. treatment centers. Only recently, in the face of the managed care challenge, have sophisticated studies been launched. Early results show that treatment is effective and offers long term economic benefits to the nation. But the data needed to make a head to head comparison between individual treatment programs is not yet available.

So—is there no trustful data with which to compare treatment programs? We think not. Our suggestion is to pay attention to your intuitive reactions and also trust the wisdom of the marketplace. Staff personnel in quality treatment centers model wellness. They should be easy to talk with, have the right answers, make you feel comfortable, and give you a sense of hope. Until we start seeing consumer reports on C.D. treatment, a reliable alternative is to ask the people who should know: previous customers. When comparing cars or stereos, it's wise to consult an owner of the vehicle or unit you're considering. "Trust the man who owns one," a popular ad used to say. This timeworn advice is valid during these fluid times in the evolution of the C.D. treatment business. Success in the marketplace is a good indicator that the service provided is of high quality.

Why Treatment Instead of Just a Twelve-Step Program?

"We have borrowed the best from medicine, psychiatry, and religion." So said Bill Wilson, the very intelligent stockbroker who co-founded A.A. And he would be the first to agree that what they borrowed was the best of those fields as of the 1930s, when the book on which A.A. is based was written. Yet much has been learned about alcoholism since then. Fifty years of more enlightened examination of this national problem and tens of millions of dollars of research have brought us a long way. More is now known about the emotional damage, the family impact, and the physiology of alcoholism.

We live in a poly-drug society today within which major value shifts have occurred since the 1930s. Much of this new knowledge and cultural change confirms the miracle of A.A. and Al-anon. At the same time, a lot of it presents new and different opportunities for earlier intervention and more rapid and higher-quality recovery.

Combining the Best

The A.A. book *Twelve Steps and Twelve Traditions* outlines the principles upon which the Alcoholics Anonymous program has evolved. Al-anon, Narcotics Anonymous, Overeaters Anonymous, and others have all adopted these same principles in practice. if not officially. The forward to the "Twelve and Twelve"—as the book is affectionately called—states, "A.A.'s Twelve Steps are a group of principles...which enable the sufferer to become happy and whole." The key word here is *enable*—defined as "to provide the means to make possible."

The early members of A.A., many of whom are still living, never intended membership in A.A. to be the total means of an alcoholic's recovery efforts. In fact, some of them were instrumental in the development of formal treatment programs for the disease. They recognized that A.A. could provide the spiritual spark needed to light the lamp of recovery; that the Twelve Steps could show the way and thus enable. But for the sufferer to become "happily and usefully whole" he must call upon the "best that medicine, psychiatry, and religion" can offer. Thus today the Twelve Steps, first developed in Alcoholics Anonymous, are the cornerstone of quality recovery from pathological dependencies and still rightfully revered as the fundamental pathway.

The self-help programs spawned from A.A. are often the first place suffering people turn for help. Nonetheless, it is an observable fact that formal treatment can accelerate and improve the quality of recovery. The visible proof of the merits of combining treatment with the twelve-step programs can be seen and heard at twelve-step group meetings. It becomes quickly obvious who has been through treatment and who has not. Most treatment "graduates" demonstrate a clearer understanding of the biogenetic nature of their disease, wrestle less with vestiges of denial, and seem more comfortable with the idea of abstinence. Those who have undergone formal treatment are quite often more in touch with their feelings and in particular have learned how to deal with anger and fear in positive ways.

Probably the most distinguishing mark of those who have experienced treatment is their clearer grasp of the family aspects of the illness. On the other hand, those who undergo treatment but do not continue in a twelve-step program appear to be missing a valuable component in their lives. It is not that they can't stay sober and drug-free without A.A., because they often do. But they seem to lack the spiritual vitality, sense of purpose, and serenity that grows out of a life based on the principles embodied in the Twelve Steps. Our acquaintance with thousands of recovered persons has convinced us that the formula for accelerated recovery and optimum wellness is this: first-class family-based treatment, including a solid aftercare component, followed by "one day at a time" living built upon the long-respected Twelve Steps of Alcoholics Anonymous.

But Whatever Happens

If attempts to intervene fail or are impossible because of broken relationships, death, dollars, or distance and if treatment for the whole family is not possible, we encourage as many as possible of those impacted to seek co-dependency treatment for themselves. They need it, deserve it, and will pay a lifetime price in emotional pain without it.

6. Follow Through After Treatment

Some experts say that 20 percent of recovery takes place in treatment and most of the rest during the first two years afterwards, providing certain aftercare steps are taken. Of all the critical actions, following through with continued recovery efforts after treatment is perhaps the most crucial to long-term success.

Aftercare is usually structured through a formal commitment by the C.D. person and family to attend professionally facilitated weekly therapy meetings in which ex-patients and their families continue to work on chemical dependency and co-dependency issues. Aftercare combined with programs such as A.A., Al-anon, and Alateen is what assures sustained recovery.

Aftercare provides the environment in which to continue processing the emotional pain of the disease. It reinforces the new beginnings in damaged relationships and helps refine valuable skills for living, such as stress management, relaxation techniques, exercise programs, nutrition, communication skills, self-esteem building, and assertiveness.

Aftercare motivates C.D. patients through the difficult early stages of establishing their twelve-step program. It is not uncommon to hear untreated A.A. members still wrestling with these issues years after quitting drinking. Similarly, recovering co-dependent people, without the benefit of aftercare, may continue suffering for years and become disillusioned because they expected the C.D. person's sobriety alone to fix all their problems. The record is clear. Those who remain faithful to their aftercare contract seldom relapse. Those who don't, often do.

Are There Exceptions?

You may feel that all Six Critical Actions are not appropriate to your situation. Maybe, but consider carefully before eliminating. Intervention, in particular, may no longer be possible. Perhaps you and the C.D. person have divorced or are now too geographically or emotionally separated for intervention to be an option. The C.D. person may be imprisoned or even dead. The other members of the family may be too dysfunctional from their own experiences in a C.D. family to be of help in your quest for recovery. We hasten to add, however, that just about all co-dependent people feel that such is the case. Oftentimes it is simply a matter of "intervening on the interveners."

Whatever your situation, it is strongly suggested that you find a source of current information, get a professional assessment, join a self-help group, and at least seriously investigate professional help. Without help it is likely that your co-dependent past will haunt your relationships and efforts at personal growth all your life. But once the steps appropriate to your circumstances are identified, there are no shortcuts. The actions we've described are the decisions and actions that have led countless others to full recovery.

Only the Beginning

The Six Critical Actions only create a climate of opportunity in which those afflicted can again reach toward their own highest potential. Full recovery demands a full lifetime commitment and a whole-person approach. Chemical dependency and co-dependency are complex pathologies that impact the entire person: body, mind, emotions, and spirit. To fully recover from its ravaging years or even decades, victims must reestablish stewardship over their bodies, profoundly revise their thinking and thought processes, achieve higher levels of emotional maturity, and find sources of strength, hope, and purpose for their lives. This demands a lifetime of personal effort and program involvement aimed at continued spiritual development, the restoration of relationships, intellectual renewal, and self-esteem building.

Practical growth steps such as smoking cessation, weight control, physical fitness, marriage counseling, and financial planning are the hallmarks of those on a true recovery path. And experience has shown that the manifold components of recovery cannot be accomplished in isolation from each other. Praying the knees out of one's pants while perched complacently on one's posterior will not do the job. Neither will frantic efforts at therapy, self-help programs, and reading all the latest books and studies without developing a spiritual dimension to one's life. There is little true health in a "recovery" characterized by smoking, poor nutrition, toxic relationships, chronic stress, depression, and lack of purpose. If the whole person is not healed, the pain is just being shifted around.

Practical Steps With a Transcendent Payoff

The end result of accomplishing these actions transcends the sum of the individual steps involved. Those who have put real energy into these efforts report a weller-than-wellness. As is the case in many natural disasters, the rebuilding process frequently produces results far more beautiful and satisfying than the original. You will hear recovered C.D. and co-dependent people make statements such as, "I'm almost glad my family got sick so we could get to where we are now." Such an utterance is hard to believe when you are at the painful front end of the process. Still, many recovering persons feel certain that their illness has offered personal growth opportunities not available to their more "fortunate" peers.

At the Very Least

Whatever else you may decide to do, take the first two suggested critical actions: Get current information and get a professional assessment of your situation. This will, at the very least, get you pointed in the direction of further help. By the time you read this book, breakthrough knowledge may be available, more effective intervention concepts discovered, and new innovative treatment models developed. For these reasons we've tried to avoid absolute statements and dogmatic pronouncements about chemical dependency and co-dependency. There has been more learned about these maladies in the last ten years than the last ten thousand. No doubt that trend will continue. There do, however, appear to be two absolutes. Abstinence and twelve-step living will be the foundation of sustained recovery for the C.D. person. And in some cases co-dependency symptoms are too deeply imprinted to be remedied by self-help alone; there is a need for professional therapy or formal treatment. These two axioms should not be tampered with lightly. But beyond those bedrock concepts, the horizons of recovery will surely expand as knowledge grows. So, simply stated, once you find your way to competent help, trust the help you get.

5

Intervention Works

"Bottoming Out"

For years it was widely accepted that C.D. persons had to "hit bottom" before they would be receptive to help. The tragedy of this notion was that people were condemned to lose everything before they could hope to recover. In the early 1960s, Vernon Johnson, an Episcopal priest who was himself recovering from alcoholism, joined with a group of enlightened and influential Minnesotans to research ways of accelerating the C.D. person's entry into treatment. Their efforts showed that "bottoming out" was a subjective perception and not an objective condition. They found that a C.D. person hit bottom and agreed to accept help when it became clear that the consequences of drinking or drugging had become too painful to bear. It wasn't that conditions were not bad enough to warrant treatment but rather that the C.D. person was too deluded to accurately appraise his own plight.

Besides dispelling the bottoming-out myth, the Minnesota group's studies of voluntary entry versus court-directed treatment of C.D. persons also produced surprising results. They found that recovery rates were about the same whether patients entered treatment voluntarily or were coerced into it. Consequently, treatment with even a minimum of willingness brought excellent chances of recovery. Johnson recognized that it was the delusion of the C.D. persons combined with enabling behavior by concerned persons that was blinding them to the severity of their condition.

He and his associates developed techniques to stop this enabling and break through the delusion long enough for the C.D. person to accept help. This win/win, nonantagonistic, nonjudgmental approach has come to be known as the Johnson Institute model of intervention. Their pioneer work was summarized in Johnson's classic book, *I'll Quit Tomorrow*. This creative approach to getting C.D. people to accept help has evolved into a wide range of approaches and techniques.

Intervention is now used in many different forms to deal with C.D. cases, not only in individual families but in business and industry, the armed forces, professional sports leagues, and the medical, legal, and other professions. Yet all these methods embody three basic components: concern; the presentation to the C.D. of documented, specific, nonjudgmental data about his drinking and drugging behavior; and an offer of help options that can be accepted with dignity. Thousands of successful interventions, using variations of this model, have shattered the myth that C.D. persons must hit bottom and lose everything. There are now proven techniques that can dramatically accelerate the time at which a C.D. person will become willing to accept help. Those who claim otherwise—and you'll no doubt encounter some who will—are simply not aware of these historical facts. There is no longer any question—intervention works.

What Intervention Is

Intervention is a sustained process, not a single event. A process consisting of education, training, counseling, and attitude changes by which concerned people can help a C.D. person to see what most everyone else can already see: that alcohol and/or other drugs have begun to dominate and damage important areas of the victim's life.

The goal of intervention is to break through the wall of delusion surrounding the C.D. person long enough to get him or her to accept help. To repeat, intervention is a win-win, nonantagonistic effort done with an absence of judgment and packaged in concern. There is no labeling, generalizing, attacking, or moralizing. Sometimes, but not always, the intervention may be in the form of a confrontational meeting with the C.D. person. Often it is simply the natural consequences of raised awareness, attitude changes, and revised communication patterns on the part of those concerned.

What Intervention Is Not

Intervention is not a case of proving the C.D. person wrong and you right or getting him to admit to being an alcoholic or drug addict. Nor is intervention a conspiracy. From the very beginning of the process, communication within the C.D. family becomes more open and honest rather than less. Whenever possible, intervention is not based upon fear, coercion, or threat of consequences but derives its power primarily from love and concern. An intervention effort conducted by a properly trained and prepared individual or group has little danger of backfiring and making the situation worse.

Intervention, as some fear, is in no way a conspiritorial, desperate, last-ditch confrontation fraught with danger and marked by fear with an all-or-nothing aura. Rather, it is a well-planned, carefully executed, proven procedure with a very high probability of success.

Who Has the Right (and the power) to Intervene?

Folklore teaches us to "mind our own business." This is certainly a tempting position to take regarding someone else's drinking or drugging. Yet, when a pathology that surrounds itself with delusion is the "business" at hand, intervention becomes a lifesaving requirement. But who has the right to step into another person's life? Any one or combination of the following power bases qualifies someone to be an intervener.

1. Love and concern for the C.D. person.

2. The C.D. person's respect for you.

3. The possession of data concerning unacceptable drinking and/or drugging behavior.

4. Leverage or clout in the C.D. person's life.

Some potential interveners may offer all 4 strengths. Others a combination of several. A few may fit only one category. But anyone meeting any of these qualifications should be considered a potential intervener.

What Makes Intervention Work?

Most persons who have lived in a C.D. situation very long can honestly say, "I've tried to intervene every way I could. He just won't listen." What is different about what we are proposing? Our approaches are based on feedback from those upon who we have successfully intervened in the past. These now recovering C.D. victims consistently report the following about their mind set prior to the intervention. First, "I had no idea it was that bad." Second, "I had no idea I was hurting so many people so much." Third, "I really didn't believe anybody still cared." And finally, "I had no idea there was a way out with dignity." Any attempt to intervene needs to hook into these unspoken needs. The techniques recommended in this chapter are designed to tap into the energy that lies within that unrevealed pain and use it to fuel the recovery process.

Two Useful Metaphors

There are two ways to view intervention that seem to help potential participants grasp the conceptual foundation of this process. The first is the notion that intervention is a martial art. A martial art of interpersonal persuasion much like judo or karate are martial arts of personal combat. The martial arts master does not confront or try to overpower nor does he bear anger or malice toward his opponent. Rather, he uses the forces at work in the other person to his advantage. Likewise, the intervener uses the anger, fear, loneliness, and hopelessness experienced by the C.D. person as the force needed to initiate recovery. This is accomplished by structuring the intervention as a win-win, non-antagonistic, non-judgmental interaction that is packaged in love and concern yet touches the pain enough to gain acceptance of a dignified help option.

A second metaphor or conceptual framework that is helpful in understanding the dynamics of intervention is that it is a grief process. Most are familiar with the idea that those suffering a loss first experience shock, then anger, then attempt to bargain with their plight, and finally—if the process is allowed to play out, come to accept the loss. Human beings go through this cycle frequently, from discovering their favorite restaurant is out of the dish they anticipated, all the way to accepting the news that they have a terminal illness and are going to die. Intervention is an effort to move the C.D. person through shock and anger to accepting the loss of a great love of their life—chemical-induced euphoria. Those who have experienced an intervention describe how they first were shocked, then angered, attempted to bargain, and then finally accepted the help offered. Such feedback would support the notion that intervention works because it facilitates the grief process the C.D. person must go through in order to accept help.

The Fundamentals

The intervention process may culminate in the courtroom, the emergency room, the living room, the boss's office—anywhere that circumstances and events combine to break through the C.D. person's delusion. Interventions can be very brief. For example, Mother says to Son in emergency room after auto accident, "Alcohol did this. Will you accept treatment now?" Son, "Yes, Mom." End of intervention. Or it can involve years of effort by a family to get all the concerned others trained and prepared to conduct a formal intervention meeting with the C.D. person. Though interventions can take many forms, it is useful to divide them into three general categories:

1. *Crisis-based intervention.* The C.D. person is offered treatment under crisis circumstances while his denial is temporarily weakened as the result of an emergency situation: D.W.I. or other arrest, marriage breakup, job loss, auto accident, medical emergency, etc.

2. *The mini-intervention.* The boss, doctor, business associate, spouse, family member, or friend alone or in a small group confronts the C.D. person about his drinking and drugging and offers help

3. *Concerned group intervention.* This highly structured intervention attempt involves as many of the significant others in the C.D. person's life as can be recruited for the process.

Expect Contingencies

Because of the volatility of the disease and the number of variables involved, intervention attempts must include planning for contingencies. Contingencies are unexpected turns such as

1. Sudden crisis (D.W.I. or other arrests, job loss, injury, illness)

2. Changes of heart (either by the C D. person or those involved in the intervention)

3. Discovery by the C.D. person that an intervention effort is in progress. (As you will see, this is not a big problem and may even be desirable.)

4. Dramatic changes in the drinking or drugging pattern. (Someone thought to be just alcoholic is discovered to be using and dealing cocaine).

These kinds of contingencies do arise in the progress of intervention efforts. Consequently, those concerned persons involved will benefit from viewing their activities as a fluid and often rapidly changing process. You may start out with an eye toward employing one of the three approaches described above (crisis-based, mini-intervention, or concerned group). But as the scenario unfolds, the actual result may be a hybrid of all three concepts. For example, if a family begins preparing for a concerned group intervention and the C.D. person is suddenly hospitalized for a serious drinking-related accident, the effort immediately shifts in the direction of a crisis-based intervention. While experiencing the immediate shock of the accident, the C.D. person may agree to go to treatment but, after recovering from his injuries, renege on the commitment. Then several of the concerned group may jump in and employ mini- intervention skills, with their individual efforts saving the day.

Such a quick turn of events is quite common in the business of intervention. But whatever the turn of events, successful efforts in all three types are marked by the presence of concern, the absence of judgment, the presentation of specific data, the application of win-win communication techniques, and the offer of help options that can be accepted with dignity.

No Guarantees But Hopeful Probabilities

No intervention counselor can guarantee that the C.D. person will come to the intervention but there is almost always a way to get him there. There is no certainty that he will listen but most usually do. They might refuse help but in most cases they accept. Treatment might not work but it more often does. Relapse may occur but if so it will probably be short-lived and signal the last gasp of the disease before real recovery begins. Still it is natural, when you've lived in a negative environment so long, to expect the worst. Yet properly prepared intervention efforts work more often than not and nearly always improve the situation even when the hoped-for outcome is delayed. In our entire professional careers we have never had a client wish they hadn't attempted to intervene.

What About Violence?

Often those contemplating an intervention attempt are worried about the possibility of a violent or suicidal reaction by the C.D. person. If there is a history or threat of violence or suicidal intentions, <u>DO NOT ATTEMPT TO INTERVENE WITHOUT COMPETENT PROFESSIONAL HELP</u>. There is no national source of data about intervention attempts. So there may well have been incidents of violence and suicide. But in the broad range of interventions we have conducted and in the several hundred we have discussed with other intervention specialists, there have been no reports of either violence or postintervention suicide attempts. When interveners are coached and prepared properly, these efforts are characterized by love, concern, dignity, respect, and hopeful help options. Such is not the stuff of which violence is born. If, however, there is a history of violence, the propriety of attempting an intervention must be seriously examined. The first priority should be your own safety and recovery. Courageous counselors may be willing to attempt an intervention with such a person. However, they know how to take special precautions, such as being sure the C.D. person is not armed, positioning him between two people strong enough to physically restrain him if necessary, seating him in a low, soft, deep chair from which it is difficult to rise, and providing easy escape routes from the room for those likely to be a target of a violent response. We had to take such measures in the case of the man described earlier who had threatened to chop off his son's head on the butcher block. We would never have involved this young man without assuring his safety. That family, incidentally, underwent treatment, and father and son have begun to work out a trusting relationship.

It's also a wise procedure to seek advice from an attorney about restraining orders or commitment actions. Arrangements should also be made for safe places for the family to relocate if necessary. This all must sound scary, so let us restate: violent reactions seldom, if ever, occur. But certainly anxiety about such responses should be raised and discussed with your intervention counselor. He or she can put your fears at rest with clear and practical guidance. If there is a history of suicide threats or attempts, certainly caution is needed to be certain any intervention effort is structured to be as loving, supportive, and hopeful as possible People don't usually respond to an outpouring of love and concerned hope with self-destructive behavior. On the other hand, doing nothing and enabling them to continue to drink and drug certainly encourages a suicidal course. We have also never encountered violence during the course of an actual intervention. In one instance a young man verbally threatened us. Fortunately for us he was sitting between his uncle and his godfather, both of whom had been All-Pro linemen in the NFL. He was a rare and foolishly brave exception.

The following chapters describe each of the three general types of interventions, with real-life examples from our case files and suggestions on how to optimize—and if necessary, combine—these approaches.

6

The Crisis-Based Intervention

Crises Are Also Opportunities

The lives of most C.D. persons eventually become one of crisis management. As the disease progresses and the C.D. person's behavior is more and more influenced by alcohol or other drugs, serious predicaments and ultimately severe crises usually unfold.

These incidents or circumstances can be fertile ground for intervention attempts. Most often these crisis-connected events are the consequences of actions while under the influence. But there is such a thing as a passive crisis as well—critical situations caused by what the C.D. person did *not* do: failing to get a promotion, not caring for his health, not paying the bills, or not meeting critical responsibilities as a spouse, parent, or citizen. In any case, crisis-based intervention is not a matter of "creating a crisis." C.D. people are quite capable of accomplishing that without assistance. Crisis-based intervention is an attempt to reinforce the adverse consequences of the crisis at a critical time and in an effective way. The object—as with all intervention efforts—is to break through the delusion long enough to get the C.D. person to accept help.

Case History—"Sharon the Terrible"

Sharon's parents came to us because their twenty-year-old daughter was in all kinds of trouble. She had written bad checks, received several D.W.I.'s, dropped out of college because of bad grades, and was running with a wild crowd. They had recently found drug paraphernalia in her room. Their one-on-one efforts to intervene were to no avail. Sharon denied she had a problem with alcohol and drugs and blamed her life problems on the poor example of her parents. They felt guilty, ashamed, and, most of all, powerless. The parents and others concerned about Sharon trained and prepared for a more structured and formal concerned group intervention. Early in the training, however, we suggested that if any crisis should suddenly occur in Sharon's life as a result of alcohol and drugs, a crisis-based intervention attempt should be made. Shortly thereafter, Sharon was seriously injured in a drinking-related automobile accident. We enlisted the help of the treating physician for data proving Sharon had been very drunk at the time of the accident and gathered facts from the arresting officer about her intoxicated behavior at the scene (she had staggered off drunkenly, even though bleeding and suffering from several broken bones and head injuries). Her mother, father, and a close friend participated in an intervention at her bedside in the hospital. Each in turn told her how much they cared about her and pointed out how alcohol was responsible for the accident and the pain it was causing Sharon, her family, and friends. They offered the opportunity to include treatment for her alcohol problem as part of total recovery from the accident. She accepted and, after her injuries were sufficiently healed, transferred to a C.D. treatment center. Sharon is sober and drug-free today.

Case History—"The Best Damn Defense Lawyer in the State"

On several occasions we have been asked to assist with interventions on "the best damn defense lawyer in the state." Since each time it was a different attorney, it would seem that C.D. defense lawyers certainly impress others with their skills. Clarence, this particular "best damn defense lawyer in the state," had been suddenly hospitalized for drinking-related health problems but was still sure that he "could handle it." Prior to the medical emergency, his wife had been preparing for a formal intervention involving a number of out-of-town friends and family members. This sudden hospitalization, however, provided a crisis-based intervention opportunity. After enlisting the treating physician, one of Clarence's law partners, and Clarence's father (himself no slouch with the scotch bottle), an intervention was done in the hospital room. The doctor stated that alcoholism was the primary cause of Clarence's secondary medical problems. That rare and courageous diagnosis, combined with the data presented by the spouse and law partner, broke through the delusion long enough for Clarence to accept transfer to a C.D. treatment center. He is sober today and the family much healthier after treatment. Of special note here is the impact an enlightened physician can have on the outcome of an intervention attempt.

Key Elements of Crisis-Based Intervention

The potency of crisis-based intervention stems from

1. Timing

2. The irrefutable nature of the crisis

3. The enlisting of powerful and objective witnesses

The intervention should be timed to take place while the C.D. person is recovering from the shock and initial trauma of whatever incident has occurred—arrest, injury, accident, broken relationship, etc.—and while still suffering the emotional consequences. In the case studies above, both C.D. persons were over the effects of anesthesia and free enough of severe pain to be lucid. But they were still scared, ashamed, and disgusted with themselves. Obviously, when a medical situation is involved, approval of the attending physician should be requested. The nature of these crisis situations is such that the evidence available is usually both objective and irrefutable and thus very difficult to resist: photos, video tapes, newspaper articles, police reports, injuries, or property damage to others, etc. The impact of evidence can be made even more powerful if the details are provided by an objective third party such as the arresting officer, attending physician, or eye witness. Because the C.D. person has such a defensive relationship with those close to him, it is often easier for him to believe information provided by someone outside the family system.

Cooperating With the Law

Several research studies suggest that some C.D. persons develop a drinking/drugging pattern that gets them in trouble with the law and some don't. And once a pattern of violence or intoxicated driving or stealing is established, it tends to continue and worsen. What this means is that allowing C.D. persons to pay the full consequences of their first brushes with the law is probably the most loving thing to do. Assisting them to "beat the rap" by providing high-powered attorneys, using political influence, or encouraging cover-ups may contribute to later and far more painful tragedy.

On the other hand, encounters with the law may offer two options for intervention. The first is passive: do nothing and permit the C.D. person to absorb the full impact of his lawbreaking behavior. This may mean a night in jail, finding and funding his own legal assistance, appearing in court alone, and facing the pain of incarceration, fines, and/or probation. This sounds cruel, but it is physical and emotional pain that fuels the recovery process. Thus, stepping in and insulating the C.D. person from the painful consequences of his intoxicated behavior may be denying him an important moment of truth as well as encouraging attitudes and behaviors with potential for dire future consequences. It's not easy to leave your kid, spouse, or sibling in jail. But very often that's the most loving thing to do.

The second option is to actively cooperate with law enforcement officers, prosecutors, and judicial officials. This might take the form of revealing the C.D. person's history of chemical dependency and asking them to offer the C.D. person the choice of treatment or prosecution. Many a C.D. person traces his recovery to such a forced choice. This kind of plea bargaining, however, needs to be approached with care and with the aid of a defense attorney experienced in such procedures. Judicial enlightenment about chemical dependency varies nationwide. It is probably accurate to assume that most judges today would rather see a C.D. person in a treatment bed than a jail cell, but that belief is not universal. So in these matters one should approach the idea of interfering in another person's legal destinies with care, discernment, and solid expert advice. But, given these cautions, we should not hesitate to exploit the potency of the law in what may be lifesaving circumstances.

What Really Is Up, Doc?

Often a medical crisis will enable a physician to intervene. Many such opportunities are lost because doctors will not risk confronting a patient's drinking or drug use unless they observe secondary symptoms like cirrhosis, gastritus, or needle infections. As discussed earlier, this reluctance may stem from the physician's own drinking or drug use, co-dependency, or lack of education and training about alcoholism and other chemical dependencies. But the most common reason physicians don't intervene more often is that they simply don't have enough data. When questioned about alcohol or drugs, C.D. patients almost always minimize or deny. So even when a problem is strongly suspected, the doctor is powerless unless some validating physical symptom is present.

Many M.D.'s are now trained to ask what are called the CAGE questions, a simple, easy-to-administer four-item test named for the symptoms it seeks to detect.

1. "Have you ever felt you should Cut down on your drinking?"

2. "Have people Annoyed you by criticizing your drinking?"

3. "Have you ever felt bad or Guilty about your drinking?"

4. "Have you ever had an Early morning drink to get rid of a hangover?"

One yes should raise suspicion. Two or more are indicators of a problem.

As a concerned friend or family member you can make the physician aware of the severity of the problem for his use in professional contacts with the C.D. person. This information can have a strong impact when discussed with the doctor, either in person or by phone, and then followed up by a letter describing your specific concerns and giving the doctor clearly stated permission to use the information.

Telling the Boss

Enlisting the C.D. person's employer in the intervention process may initially sound like economic suicide. "If I tell the boss, he'll lose his job" is a typical and valid apprehension. But of course if he doesn't quit drinking and/or drugging, he'll get fired anyway. No question about it, going to the boss is a tricky business. But it also might be just what's needed to push the C.D. person into help.

Here are a few ideas on this very sensitive subject. A less threatening starting place is to call (or have a confidant call) the employer and—without revealing identities—speak to the personnel manager or whoever acts in that capacity. Inquire about the organization's policy regarding employee alcohol or other drug problems and the availability of a formal employee assistance program. Should there be an official program, contact the program director—still anonymously—and find out how it works. If you become convinced that confiding in the program director (or one of the program staff to whom you may be referred) is a positive step, then take the risk. He or she can explain company policies, recommend help resources, clarify insurance benefits, and in some instances actually participate in the intervention effort. If there is no formal program or you just don't trust the response, at least ask the question—"What happens if one of your employees goes into treatment for alcohol or drug use?" The answer to that question can help you decide whether you want to involve anyone from the workplace.

What If He Is the Boss?

One of the most effective and commonly encountered defenses in C.D. people is overachievement on the job. "How can I be an alcoholic? I'm the best man in the outfit!" is a common utterance when C.D. persons are confronted. Since that is often true, C.D. people are frequently situated on lofty professional or corporate perches and not accountable to many others. Even so, there are usually business partners, professional peers, legal advisors, corporate physicians, and boards of directors who have power and influence over the C.D. person. When the C.D. person is the boss, such power brokers may well be your most forceful allies, especially if the C.D. person's behavior is an economic threat to them. Everybody is accountable to somebody.

When to Involve the Workplace

There is no clear-cut guide as to whether and when to enlist help from the boss, co-workers, the company doctor, or the employee assistance program in the intervention process. But when an alcohol- or drug- related crisis has either become known at work or is affecting job performance, the secret is already out. So you might as well pursue the help that may lie in the hands of those at work who still care. This can get complicated, because supervisors and co-workers can also be enablers. Just like family members, they may have been covering up, lying, and making excuses for the C.D. person. They too can be reluctant to confront someone else's drinking or drug use because of their own. But if a real crisis occurs that will affect job performance—arrest, unacceptable absenteeism, serious injury, public embarrassment, professional licensing problems, damage to corporate reputation, or product or consumer liability—the organization is already involved. Therefore, you might as well enlist its help to intervene. Your alcohol and drug abuse counselor, personal attorney, and Al-anon sponsor/group members can be of assistance in making these decisions.

Semper Paratus

The next two chapters cover the two most common forms of intervention: the mini-intervention and the concerned group. But as you begin pursuing the skills needed for those kinds of approaches, a crisis may erupt. So, as you gather the forces and seek the counseling and training needed for a more formal and structured intervention effort, be ready to act quickly and decisively in an unexpected emergency. Don't worry about "doing it right." Just get to the C.D. person, tell him you care, point out what has happened because of drinking and/or drugging, and ask if he'd be willing to accept some help. Assure the C.D. that you know he is not bad, stupid, or crazy but that the present situation makes it mighty obvious that he has a diseased relationship with alcohol or drugs— and that help is available. Remind him of friends or public figures he admires who have undergone similar treatment. Emphasize that now—while the pain of the present crisis is fresh in his mind—is the time to decide to end the pain for himself and those who care. Will it help? More people probably enter help under these circumstances than any other. When the D.A. is breathing down their necks, the doctor is staring at them over the still-damp X-rays, or the boss is offering them one more chance, C.D. persons often experience instant enlightenment. As one recovered sage once said, "I didn't have a spiritual awakening. I had a rude awakening." Crisis-based interventions are very powerful and should be attempted whenever circumstances offer an opportunity.

7

The Mini-Intervention

It's Tough

One concerned person alone confronting a C.D. person is the most tried and least successful way to intervene. These mini-intervention efforts certainly don't fail for lack of concern or effort. But the underlying dynamics of these confrontations doom most such attempts. Unless the confronting person has special training and preparation, the conversation usually degenerates into generalities and accusations such as "You've turned into a drunk and you're ruining our marriage." To which the C.D. person replies with a full array of defensive and manipulative skills. By the time the change is over, the confronter often feels guilty for having raised the subject and is convinced that a lot of the drinking or drugging is his or her fault. These highly charged and often argumentative and judgmental encounters can be refined and made useful, however, if certain ground rules are followed and a few simple skills practiced.

The mini-intervention approach has an important place in the overall intervention scheme. For, although one such confrontation by itself is seldom effective, there often is a positive and cumulative result when conducted on a frequent and recurring basis. The C.D. person's delusion and denial can be gradually undermined when many of those who care about him stop enabling, break the no-talk rules, and consistently hold him accountable for his behavior under the influence.

Safety First—Yours!

When there is a history or threat of physical violence, any intervention effort should be approached with great caution and in certain cases avoided. *Your personal safety and that of your family and friends is the first priority.* Remember, C.D. persons are capable of acts under the influence of the chemical that grossly violate their sober values. This not infrequently includes violent acts against loved ones. If physical harm is a concern, get competent professional advice before attempting intervention. *If violence occurs, get out…get protection…get legal advice.* You can do that by temporarily fleeing to a safe place (the home of a relative or friend or a community shelter), reporting the incident to the police, and discussing the situation with an attorney. Keep in mind that you didn't cause the abuse and you can't fix it. If you can't afford a lawyer, contact the legal aid society. Sadly, there is a lot of family violence these days. Overworked police can sometimes get a bit apathetic about these domestic situations. At the same time, being physically battered literally beats down your ability to reach out for help. This combination of police overload and victim reluctance can be deadly. We urge as powerfully as we can: *if someone is physically hurting you, CRY FOR HELP UNTIL YOU GET IT!!!* It is unwise to return to an abusive C.D. person until he has gotten help and a professional advises that it is safe to renew the relationship. These self-protection actions may sound scary at a time when you are already quite fearful. Nonetheless, there is no benefit from keeping yourself or loved ones in harm's way in an attempt to "save" the C.D. person. On the contrary, many C.D. people have found their way to treatment and recovery by way of the shock of loved ones leaving and the police arriving. Put yourself on top of your own priority list.

But If It's Safe

When physical harm is not a threat, every drinking or drugging bout can be an opportunity for mini-intervention. Such a confrontation might sound something like this: "Shirley, I am very concerned about you. Last night when I came home, you seemed to be asleep on the couch in the clothes you'd worn to work. When I tried to awaken you, I could smell alcohol on your breath, and you didn't respond when I tried to talk to you. A drink had been spilled on the floor, and the stub of a joint was in the ashtray. Both the kids were in their beds crying. Joey told me you sent them to their room after picking them up at the nursery at 5:30. He said you promised them dinner in a little while. It was 10:00 and they still hadn't eaten. The baby had spread the contents of her dirty diaper all over her clothes and face and had pulled the nipple off her bottle and spilled it all over the mess. Joey kept repeating through his tears, 'Mommy must be dead, she won't wake up. Mommy must be dead, she won't wake up.' He was terrified, and the baby was purple-faced from hours of screaming. I was angry, scared, and disgusted. Shirley, I know how much you love the kids and that you would never behave this way if you hadn't been drinking and smoking pot. Please, get some help."

Notice that the above statement is very specific, contains no labels or moral judgments, and yet holds the C.D. person responsible for her behavior and its emotional impact on others.

Developing a Core Message

Mini-interventions seem frightening because past experience has taught us to expect anger, denial, and all the other defenses and manipulations that accompany this disease. The result is often to wish we had not raised the subject, or even leaves us feeling that the whole mess is our fault. Take a lesson from the politicians. Candidates and office holders today hire media consultants to teach them how to keep interviews focused on their agenda and not that of the interviewer; they develop what is termed a core message. Questions asked or arguments raised receive a brief response and then they bridge to their core message. You can apply the same skill to your mini-intervention attempts. Your core message should sound something like this:

"Joe, I'm very concerned about you. Last night I saw you gulping drinks at the boss's dinner party. Later, you told that awful joke about the bullfighter. Nobody laughed. They just stared in disbelief. I heard your boss mutter, 'There goes the office drunk again. We're going to have to do something about him.' I know how much your job means to you, Joe. There is a program here in town that can help us with the way alcohol is affecting our lives. All I have to do is call and set up an appointment for an assessment. Will you go with me?"

When Joe responds, "My boss is an old prude. I was just having a good time," or some other alibi or excuse, don't get hooked into an argument. Bridge to your core message.

"Maybe he is. Still, I am very concerned and I know you wouldn't have embarrassed yourself if you hadn't been drinking. You value your job too much. There is a program here in town etc., etc., etc."

You can avoid argument and maintain win-win dynamics with this technique. So compose and mentally rehearse your core message. The content will vary from time to time but the outline is the same: concern—a description of the drinking/drugging behavior—there is help—let's go. Having a well rehearsed core message is the key to effective mini-intervention attempts. This technique takes much of the fear out of confronting the C.D. person with his chemically induced behavior. It also keeps the message of hope and help in the forefront of your relationship.

Timing

The C.D. person will be most receptive to these intervention efforts during the "morning after"—when sober or at least less under the influence and yet suffering a hangover, remorse, or fear of the consequences of recent chemically induced behavior. Physical and emotional pain is almost always what motivates the C.D. person to accept help. These one-on-one scenes can be a powerful means to bring that pain into the consciousness of the victim. Individually, such attempts will seldom penetrate the C.D. person's well-developed defenses. But when done with love and concern as each opportunity presents itself, these efforts can have a cumulative impact on the delusion and denial surrounding the disease. Finally, remember that not saying anything to C.D. persons regarding their aberrant behavior enables them to stay blinded by delusion and allows the disease to progress. And as this progression advances, intervention becomes more and more difficult. So the time to act is yesterday. If you don't act soon, there literally may be no tomorrow.

Peer Intervention Programs

If the one about whom you are concerned is a licensed professional, some powerful assistance may be available to you. Most professions—physicians, attorneys, dentists, pharmacists, nurses, veterinarians, airline pilots, and others—have what are called impaired professional or peer assistance programs. The strength of these activities varies from occupation to occupation and state to state. The best of them employ well trained volunteer interventionists from the profession who carry the clout of possible license suspension if the C.D. person refuses to accept treatment. Call the state association for the profession in question and ask to speak to the person who manages their peer assistance program. Remain anonymous until you feel comfortable with the help they offer. Assistance can range from a briefing on the profession's policies when a C.D. member undergoes treatment all the way to aiding in the organizing and conduct of the intervention itself. Our work includes conducting training courses for prospective interveners in these peer assistance programs in many parts of the country. We know first hand that many of them are well organized and offer invaluable help. If this applies, be sure to check it out.

On the Job

Mini-interventions are especially useful and effective in the work setting. The implied threat of adverse job action if help is not accepted can have a powerful impact. If you are reading this book because you're the employer, supervisor, or manager of a once-valued employee whose attendance, performance, or behavior on the job is deteriorating, C.D. or co-dependency is the likely culprit. Is it appropriate to intervene? You bet. What employees do off the job is none of your business. But attendance, performance, and behavior at work is your business. On that basis you have a right to intervene. First, check with the personnel office to see whether the company has an organized employee assistance program. If so, call the program coordinator and follow his or her advice. If there is no established program, you may wish to attempt to intervene yourself.

When you do, don't try to diagnose the problem. Stick to documented examples of attendance, performance, and/or behavior problems. Don't judge, moralize, label, or argue. Simply state the case and offer help options. If challenged, use concern as your justification for intervening.

Developing the Necessary Skills

Several years ago we developed a device to help keep these on-the-job interventions on track. It's called the REACH outline. It has proven helpful in staying organized and taking the fear out of workplace and other one-on-one confrontations.

Many managers and supervisors to whom we have taught this REACH approach reported the outline to be very useful. Keep in mind that an employee cannot usually be forced to accept treatment. But it can be made clear that if things don't change for the better, there will be consequences to their continued unacceptable attendance, performance, or behavior.

R — eason	"The reason for this meeting is..."
E — valuation	State the specific attendance, performance, and/or behavior problems.
A — lternatives	"As your supervisor, here are my alternatives..." (Spell out the specific help that is available and the company policies regarding insurance coverage, time off work, etc.) Then point out what the company policy will be if the unacceptable attendance, performance, and behavior does not improve within a specific time period.
C — oncern	Emphasize that concern for the person is a primary motive for this confrontation.
H — ope	Point out the reasons for the employee to be hopeful that help does work and all can be well.

Mini-intervention attempts can be made more effective by the acquisition of certain attitudes and communication skills. These abilities are also embodied in the more elaborate and structured concerned group intervention described in the next chapter. If you can master the techniques demanded by this approach, you have automatically learned the skills needed for all three. Consequently, we recommend that anyone faced with the possibility of an intervention refer to procedures and skills covered in detail in Chapter 8.

8

The Concerned Group
Intervention

Love Does Conquer All

Love and concern are the most powerful forces in any intervention attempt. And the love and concern of many is even more powerful. Consequently, a group of family, friends, co-workers, and professional peers who care about the C.D. person collectively possess the greatest potential for successful intervention. Such an approach is called a concerned group intervention. Typically it is a very structured effort involving considerable preparation and training. Concerned group interventions have been successful when led by one of the significant participants. However, the likelihood of success is enhanced when the effort is conducted under the guidance of a specially qualified professional. The concerned group intervention may be defined as follows: *a meeting with a C.D. person in which as many significant others as possible, after careful preparation, present specific but nonjudgmental examples of behavior-under-the-influence that conflict with the C.D. person's values, report the pain it has caused them; and offer options that the C.D. person can accept with dignity.*

There is no official, national intervention scorekeeper. However, our professional contact with intervention counselors around the country indicates that efforts of this type have at least a 70 percent probability of ending with the C.D. person agreeing to enter treatment, either immediately or within a few days. As of this writing, we have personally facilitated nearly 500 such attempts and over 90 percent of the C.D. persons took the help offered. In the situations that "didn't work," either important people in the C.D. person's life could not or would not participate, the data presented were not powerful enough, or certain "concerned" persons sabotaged the effort because—for financial, business, or personal reasons—they did not want the C.D. person to get well. Perhaps more notable than the few failures are the many concerned groups who never needed to hold the formal intervention. The changes they made in their relationship with the C.D. person as a result of preparing for the intervention resulted in circumstances that led him to accept help. Getting ready for the intervention shows that the best way to change someone else's behavior is to begin by changing your own.

Finding Power

Feeling powerless is a logical state of affairs for a C.D. family. Believing that you've tried everything possible and yet seeing all efforts fail produces a sense of futility. Consequently, desperation rather than enlightenment drives most C.D. families to seek "outside" help. This is ironic because the power to intervene really lies "inside" the system of family and friends that surrounds the C.D. person. It is the emotional pain suffered by those who love the C.D. person that fuels the intervention process. The C.D. person has learned to control the feelings of those around him and manipulate their behavior. As long as this power is granted, little can be done to change the situation. But by breaking the no-talk rules, confronting the unacceptable behaviors, taking back control of your own feelings, and getting help for yourselves, the spark of intervention can be lit. The key point is that the power to intervene is internal to the concerned group rather than some magic external force brought to bear by a counselor. The intervention process simply converts the negative emotional energy in the C.D. family and friends into a positive force that drives the healing process. It's you who has the raw power! All that is needed is guidance on how to channel and use it.

A Proven Formula

Over the years we have modified and refined our particular formula for the concerned group intervention into a rather rigid series of steps which, when followed, produced a very high record of success. To the extent that it becomes necessary to change or depart from this proven approach, the likelihood of the C.D. person accepting help will be lessened. The intervention process, as we define it, involves three phases of activity: planning and coordinating, training and preparation, and intervention and follow-through. Accordingly, we will describe each of these phases and pass on suggestions learned from our experiences in real-life interventions.

Phase One: Planning and Coordinating

Find a Competent Counselor

You'll need trained help in dealing with a chemically dependent family member, friend, employee, or co-worker. *Act. Do it now!* Call a local alcohol or drug program or agency and ask about intervention counselors and programs. If that's too scary, *right now* call someone to whom you've turned in the past: physician, counselor, attorney, clergy person, etc. Don't ask them to help you intervene, if they could have, they already would have. Just ask them to steer you to someone or someplace that might understand intervention. When you do make contact with a potential intervention counselor, ask whether he or she is trained and experienced with the Johnson Institute model of intervention. Professionals with the proper training will be familiar with this term. Take the time to find an intervention counselor experienced with this model. It works.

The best and most successful intervention counselors have a unique combination of skills and background. First of all, they have current knowledge about chemical dependency and how it affects individuals and families. The intervention counselor must be able to penetrate the manipulation, controlling, and intimidation and see instead a diseased person full of emotional pain and desperately in need of help. At the same time, the counselor must be aware that the wall of defensive behavior, delusion, and denial surrounding the C.D. person must be breached or he may die—certainly spiritually and often physically.

Beyond just understanding this illness and the plight of its victims, the intervention counselor must possess the charisma and leadership skills required to corral as many as a dozen or more concerned people, all of whom are to some extent suffering co-dependency symptoms. To mold such a confluence of frequently opposed agendas into a unified, trained, and motivated intervention group is a high-order challenge. So the intervention counselor must be educator, therapist, coach, and, to a large extent, salesperson—salesperson because a high level of persuasive communication skills on the part of the counselor can be of great value during the closing moments of an intervention. Sometimes, when the data presented don't quite break through the C.D. person's delusion, a respectful, nonantagonistic, win/win dialogue between the counselor and the C.D. person can overcome objections and save the day. When you seek out professional intervention assistance, look for experience, emotional maturity, and a track record of successful interventions.

Arrange a Professional Intervention Planning Conference

Before involving many others in the process, one or two of the primary concerned persons should meet with the intervention counselor to sort out the problem, decide on courses of action, identify potential interveners, and plan the intervention effort. At this meeting one of the interveners is usually appointed as the single point of contact for all future communications and coordination concerning the intervention. Keep attendance at this gathering down to two or three key players—usually the person who initiated the idea and one other trusted concerned person. The purpose is to break the no-talk rules, gain an accurate picture of the situation, identify all potential interveners, develop the strategies and schedules needed to get everyone trained and prepared, decide on a treatment program, and select at least a tentative time and place for the actual intervention.

Recruit and Motivate Interveners

Under the guidance of the counselor, potential interveners are contacted and enlisted to participate in the intervention process. The core of this group is usually family members and close friends, but may include ex-spouses, disliked in-laws, "fragile" family members, young children, distant relatives, long-lost friends, and others who may be difficult to recruit but nonetheless represent potent interveners. This step is not easy. Chemically dependent families are often geographically and emotionally separated. Because of their own co-dependency, some family members or friends may be unwilling or unable to participate. So frequently it is necessary to "intervene on the interveners"—that is, design strategies to gain the support of key persons who are resistant. Some may just need a bit of reassurance and encouragement from the intervention counselor. Others will respond after receiving more current information. But some may require tough confrontation to break through their own denial. Such challenges in pulling together an intervention are the rule, not the exception. Families seldom march into the counselor's office arm-in-arm, possessed with unity of purpose and high motivation saying, "Murphy family reporting for intervention duty." In reality, most families considering intervention are divided, scared, confused, and full of doubt. Assistance will be needed to meld them into a cohesive and effective intervention team. Experienced intervention counselors know how to do this. We are reminded of a politician's wife who was so "devoted" that the other concerned persons were afraid to involve her in the intervention effort. Because she was sensitive to her husband's political aspirations, her friends were worried she would blow the whistle. The strategy employed was for two of them to invite her for breakfast at a restaurant near the hotel where the intervention group was to train and prepare. At the breakfast, she was invited "to a meeting of friends discussing her husband's political future." She accepted. At the meeting the concerned persons told her that he had no political future unless his alcoholism was arrested. Since they were his primary fund-raisers, she listened, stayed, and played a crucial role in the intervention. This is what is meant by intervening on the interveners.

What About the Kids?

Consistently, we've observed children to have strong impact in an intervention. Yet the natural and understandable desire of older family members is to protect the kids. But that is much like trying to protect them from a storm by pretending it isn't out there. The children have heard the thunder and seen the lightning of this family disturbance and know much more about what is going on than adults suspect or wish to admit. More importantly, kids are feeling the emotional pain and need help as much as anyone in the family system. They need to talk about these sights and sounds, and the intervention is a good place to start. Follow the advice on this matter of the professional with whom you are working. But we have seen young children powerfully impact the C.D. person with a therapeutic result for the youngsters as well. For example, a six-year-old daughter revealed how her alcoholic father kept a pan next to his chair in which to throw up. After doing so, he would make her empty it. Kids need to talk about these awful realities. When unable to, they will turn them painfully inward and carry the damage into adulthood.

Phase Two: Training and Preparation

Attend an Education Program

The identified and recruited intervention participants need to attend an education program that provides an update on chemical dependency, its impact on families, and the principles of intervention. Public education about intervention is now found in almost any major community. Often these programs are presented as a free service by agencies such as the local council on alcoholism and drug abuse. Many treatment centers also sponsor community education on these subjects. Programs that present mock interventions or include films or video tapes portraying intervention scenes are especially valuable. Check the public service announcements in the local newspaper, call the council on alcoholism and drug abuse, or query the treatment centers usually listed in the Yellow Pages under "Alcoholism Information and Treatment Centers."

Get Help for Co-Dependency

Intervention training often gets interveners in touch with their own co-dependency. Participants suffering from the pains of co-dependency are strongly encouraged, at the very least, to seek help from a support group such as Al-anon, Adult Children of Alcoholics, Tough Love Parents, etc. Since just about everyone who has an emotional bond with a C.D. person suffers from some co-dependency, it's a good idea for all participants to get an evaluation from the counselor as to the propriety of seeking therapy for co-dependency.

Untreated co-dependent people can sabotage the intervention. They bring with them defensive behaviors; the controlling, the attention-getting tactics, the inappropriate humor, or the silence of fear. If these issues are not being dealt with in venues separate from the intervention, then valuable time and energy will be wasted during intervention, preparation. Intervention facilitators must help participants break through their own delusion and denial in order to recall the C.D.'s unacceptable behavior. That is more easily accomplished if the participants are already in a "safe" system and getting the help they need for their own pain and defenses. If you have lived around a C.D. person for any length of time at any time in your life, you will benefit from help and you deserve it.

Break the No-Talk Rules

It is essential to create an atmosphere of openness, trust, and honesty within the intervention group. This may require free discussion of previously taboo events and subjects and the putting aside of long-standing differences. C.D. people, by virtue of chemically induced behavior and sophisticated defense systems, will often perpetrate an array of intrigues, secret alliances,triangles (sexual and otherwise), bizarre incidents, and other "delicate" situations. Not surfacing and processing such data early can lead to unexpected surprises that may sabotage the intervention effort and/or the concealment of valuable information. Family members are often reluctant to discuss these sensitive matters, believing they are the only ones who know. This is seldom the case, but these extreme examples of behavior-in-conflict-with-values make for the most powerful kinds of intervention statements.

For the C.D. person to see the severity of his condition, he must experience the emotional consequences of his worst drinking and/or drugging behaviors. To touch that pain demands breaking the no-talk rules and presenting the truth, no matter how uncomfortable that may be.

A classic case in our files involves a woman's sexual indiscretion. During the phase of intervention training in which the concerned persons were writing their statements, a male friend of the family came to us privately. He described how, in the course of a pool party at his home, the woman being intervened upon had gotten very drunk and seduced him behind the cabana. The friend had himself been intoxicated enough to temporarily put aside the fact that he was supposed to be her husband's best friend. To his credit, however, he was willing to break the no-talk rules and bring up this incident, but he feared it would embarrass the husband and children. A while later, the woman's thirteen-year-old son furtively approached us, relating the same incident. It seems he was spending the night with the party host's son and witnessed Mom's indiscretion from a balcony above the pool. The young man felt sure his mother would never do such a thing sober and wanted to tell her this in the intervention—except he didn't want to hurt his father. By now you have probably guessed who appeared next: Dad. But he, of course, wanted to protect the son and his friend. This tale demonstrates that, if one person is brave enough to come forward with an incident in which the C.D. person grossly violated his own values while under the influence, others will corroborate and give permission to use it. This kind of powerful specific data is vital to breaking through the deadly delusion that surrounds the C.D. person.

Write Intervention Statements

The concerned group will be coached on how to compose two or three very specific, hard-hitting but nonjudgmental written statements that point out powerful examples of the C.D. person's unacceptable drinking and/or drugging behavior. The use of written rather than extemporaneous intervention statements is strongly recommended. Unscripted interventions tend to quickly degenerate into win-lose, antagonistic, argumentative battles. It takes a while to come up with effective intervention statements. One older woman came to our information program several times. She told us that her drinking husband never did anything "bad." She couldn't grasp the notion that it was what he wasn't doing that was "bad." He was no longer husband, father, lover, friend; he just quietly drank. We ran into her months later. She told us through tear-filled eyes, "He finally did something bad. One night he died."

If you have trouble recalling incidents, think about ruined holidays, birthdays, anniversaries, kid's important school or sports functions, dangerous driving behavior, broken promises, blackouts, sexual impotency, physical and emotional abuse, missed work, passing out, throwing up, staying out all night, losing the car, or failure to perform as a spouse, parent, citizen, friend, worker. In other words, things the C.D. person did in ways he really didn't want to or things he really wanted to do but failed to do. At first such incidents may be difficult to remember. Talk with the others about your history with the C.D. person. Break the no-talk rules, and eventually hard-hitting statements will emerge. Write them down in the following format:

Intervention Statement Outline

1. *Concern:* State your love and/or concern for the C.D. person.

2. *Incident:* Describe in specific detail an incident in which the C.D. person did something under the influence that seriously violated his own values. Give dates, times, places, graphic portrayals, sounds, smells, expressions—exactly what happened.

3. *Evidence:* Provide proof that chemicals were involved in the incident, such as "I saw you drink three double scotches before we left the house. You then had a double martini before dinner and two glasses of wine with your meal, followed by two brandies."

4. *Feelings:* Describe how being a witness or participant in the incident made you feel—sad, terrified, sick to your stomach, angry, hurt, discounted, unloved, disappointed.

5. *Concern:* Close with another statement of concern.

The following statements have been used in various actual interventions:

> I love you, John. Last Friday at 4 p.m, you called from the office and said you wanted to take me out for dinner and to be ready at 6 p.m. I dressed in the blue suit you said you liked so much and looked forward to the evening as I waited for you to arrive. I waited and waited, and finally at 11 p.m. I went to bed, not knowing what had happened and feeling disappointed, angry, and very scared. At 3 a.m. I heard banging on the front door and someone rattling the doorknob. I got up just in time to see you fall into the living room and grab at the couch for support. You stared at me with your eyes like slits and your jaw clenched, and thundered through slurred speech, "What the hell are you staring at?" I could smell the alcohol across the room and saw the red, glazed eyes. You pushed past me and

sprawled onto the bed, fully clothed. I felt frightened, angry, and very alone.

When I approached you the next morning about what had happened, you did not recall anything and said, "You made that up. It wasn't that bad." I am very scared and feel so powerless. I am so concerned.

Mom, I love you a lot. Last month my friends came over for my birthday. We were in my room listening to records when you walked into the room dressed in your slip. You started dancing around the room to the music and slurred, "Aren't we having fun, fun, fun?" I could smell the alcohol on your breath and watched with dread as you whirled unsteadily around the room. I was so embarrassed. I didn't know what to do. My feet seemed glued to the floor. My friends scampered out of the house, laughing as they ran. I wanted to die. I wish I had my sober mom back.

Mom, I love you. Last Wednesday you said you would pick me up from school and I waited and waited for over an hour and you didn't come. I decided I had better walk home, and when I got there I found you on your bed, eyes half open, smelling of alcohol, clothes disheveled. I tried to wake you but you didn't wake up. You had threatened to kill yourself before, and this time I was afraid you had. I kept crying, "Mom, I love you. Mom, I love you," till your eyes opened wide and I knew you were alive. Please get help, Mom. I love you.

Jack, I care about you. We have no physical relationship anymore. Friday night I tried to set up a romantic evening. I fixed a candlelight dinner and arranged for the children to be at the movie. You came home in a good mood, smiling and happy, and held me as though you really cared. We had dinner and I played some of our favorite music. You insisted on having more and more wine, and as you drank, you changed. You talked over and over about what a son of a bitch your boss was and stopped paying any attention to me. I tried to get you to dance with me and you said, "You're too old to dance. You don't know any of the new dances like the girls at the club do." I was so hurt. I went into the kitchen and cried. Later on, you said you wanted me to make love to you. By then you smelled bad and were slurring your words and staggering. When we went to bed, you couldn't make love, Jack. You were unable to. You were impotent, Jack. I care about you so much.

I am terribly worried about you, Jim. When you were younger, you were always reading about ships and the sea. So often you would talk about going to Annapolis and becoming a naval officer. During your first two years in high school your grades were tops and you wrote our congressman about an appointment to the Academy. Beginning last semester your grades dropped, your good friends Bob and Dave stopped coming around, and you began to skip studying and to stay out late. Last week, while doing the laundry, your mother found marijuana remnants in your jeans pockets. Then Saturday night you bumped your car into the garage door and were weaving as you came up the walk. You had trouble getting your key in the door. I opened it and could smell alcohol on your breath. You said in a high-pitched voice, "Hi, Pop. How the f _ _ _ are you?" You fell into my arms and I had to help you to bed. The next day you couldn't remember where you'd been or the scene at the door. I see alcohol and drugs destroying your dream, and I feel sad, scared, and powerless. We've found a program that can help you. Please accept the help we offer.

Note the absence of judgment, moralizing, labeling, and generalities. The idea is to create a win/win, nonantagonistic, concerned, and loving atmosphere. If the intervention effort feels conspiratorial, accusative, or otherwise negative, the statements should be refined and revised until the net impact of listening to all the statements seems loving and nonjudgmental.

Concerned Group Work Sessions

Preparing for a formal intervention will require attendance at working meetings conducted by the intervention counselor(s) during which participants refine their draft statements, coordinate schedules, assign responsibilities, and rehearse. Get together as many times as needed to be certain each participant's statements are as potent and well composed as possible. It is helpful to view the situation this way: If all the statements were put in a hat and the C.D. person were to draw just one, would that single statement have the power to intervene? Such is an impossible goal, but it is a good target.

Follow the suggestions of the intervention counselor for edits, changes, and word choices; his or her experience is the best guide. Keep working on and refining the statements, but don't waste time and money arguing with the counselor. Intervention is not an exact science nor entirely an intuitive art, and you'll find that the counselor's professional experience is usually the best guide. Considerable time and effort is required to write, revise, edit, and fine-tune intervention statements. But once this work is done, leave well enough alone. Excessive revision and rehearsing will bring on staleness and rob the process of emotional power.

Gather for a Final Preparation Meeting

In this final session the intervention statements are critiqued one last time. The group then role-plays the intervention. This gives the participants an opportunity to feel the power of their combined statements, which removes some of the fear and apprehension. The practice session also assists the intervention counselor(s) in determining the sequence in which participants should read their statements, where they should sit in relation to each other and to the C.D. person, and other logistics. Subjects to be discussed at this meeting might include making treatment arrangements, escorting the C.D. person to the treatment facility, packing his bag, arranging for time off work, caring for the cats and dogs, or any other obstacles that might surface. The date, time, and place of the intervention attempt are determined along with logistics such as where participants will park and who will invite—and perhaps escort—the C.D. person to the meeting. Any remaining doubts, concerns, and "what ifs" are resolved. It is our custom to end this final gathering by having all join hands in a circle and then praying or meditating—whatever is your preference—in order to instill a sense of closure and unity.

Once we encountered a rather cynical power-broker type during an intervention on a very powerful political figure. Upon completion of the final preparation meeting, we led this joining of hands. From the look on his face, he obviously viewed this ritual as foolish and unnecessary. The touch-and-go but eventually successful intervention involved a group of fifteen family members, friends, and political allies and one very tough and highly resistant C.D. politician. Afterward, the cynic came to us and said, "When you had us join hands together last night I felt silly and questioned the need for such a device with mature people. But today, when it looked as if things were going badly, I remembered the feeling of being all together in this effort and it gave me great strength." Moral: trust the counselor. He or she may know you and the situation better than you think.

Deal With the What Ifs

Last-minute doubts, apprehensions, and fears of those preparing for a formal intervention attempt need to be resolved. What if...he won't show up...arrives under the influence...flees after seeing the group...gets angry or violent...breaks down in tears...argues...refuses help...cuts them off financially? Won't he lose his job...be embarrassed publicly...hate us for doing this...feel that we ganged up and conspired...seek revenge? Isn't this disloyal, unfair, downright sneaky? The answers to these concerns and many other such "what ifs" could fill a book. In general, the response to all these questions is contained in the key words of the definition for a concerned group intervention: *A meeting of concerned persons with a chemically dependent person at which specific nonjudgmental examples of drinking—or drugging-related behavior—which was in conflict with his own values—is presented in an atmosphere of concern, after which help options are offered that the C.D. person can accept with dignity.* Such a confrontation is a loving act. By its very nature a professionally facilitated concerned group intervention should produce a calm, nonthreatening, business-like scene. It is an "everybody wins" proposition in which the C.D. person receives a great deal of love and concern—only his behavior is attacked.

The data presented simply prove how an otherwise good, intelligent, sane human being is doing a lot of self-defeating things that cause an enormous amount of pain in himself and those he professes to love. There is no judging, labeling, personal attacking, anger, or other provocative behavior. Throughout a properly conducted intervention, the C.D. person's dignity is respected and his worth affirmed. If properly trained, participants will realize they are part of a life-saving endeavor. Furthermore, if the participants have joined a support group or sought other help for their co-dependency issues, they will have heard many of these "what if" situations discussed by fellow recovering family members who have already been involved in an intervention.

Trust the Professional(s)

Intervention counselors should have reassuring answers to most of these concerns. If the one you employ doesn't, get somebody else. Trained professionals will have strategies for getting the C.D. person to come to the meeting. They will know how to arrange the room, seat the people, engender a willingness on the part of the C.D. person to listen, determine the sequence in which statements are presented, handle objections raised by the C.D., prevent or deal with violence, and so on. Find a good intervention counselor and then trust the one you find.

What If He Won't Come to the Meeting?

He always does, but just about everyone preparing for an intervention worries about this possibility. A proven approach is as follows: Identify the person within the intervention group who has the most positive or least antagonistic relationship with the C.D.

person. Have that designated messenger call the C.D. person and issue an invitation that sounds something like, "I need to talk to you about matters involving you that concern the entire family. Would you please meet with me at (intervention location/ date/ time)?" If the C.D. person asks for details, the messenger remains vague but does not lie. The response might be: "It's a confidential matter that I'd rather not discuss on the phone, but it is something very important and I really need your participation. Please come!" Of course, the C.D. person will suspect something is up, especially if many of those concerned have recently accelerated and strengthened their mini-intervention attempts. And that's O.K. It is not necessary for the intervention to come as a total surprise in order to be effective. What those who have been intervened upon tell us later is that, yes, they knew something was going on but realized it would be difficult to avoid the meeting. Besides, they were curious and, in addition, felt confident of being able to handle whatever it was all about. After all, they had been manipulating and controlling this bunch for years. Why should this be any different?

What If He Flees?

Won't the C.D. person turn around and leave when he sees the concerned group? It's only happened to us twice. Once the C.D. person walked out and went into treatment on his own a few days later. Another time we went after the person and convinced her to return. However, to head off this contingency, we now designate someone in the group to go after the C.D. person should he attempt to leave. The person explains that this is a gathering of people who love him and simply want to discuss some matters of concern. Having such a contingency plan is reassuring to those involved, but here is no absolute guarantee that the C.D. person will return and listen.

Phase Three: The Intervention Phase

This Is It!

This is the actual meeting with the C.D. person at which the statements are read and help is offered. If the C.D. person accepts, he is taken directly from the intervention site to the treatment facility where arrangements have been made. Here is what it is like.

Typical Intervention Scene

The C.D. person is escorted into the room. The concerned persons are seated in a loose circle, with empty seats available for the C.D. person and the escort. Everybody is scared stiff, including any rational intervention counselor. As they enter the circle, a respected member of the group, who may be the escort, introduces the C.D. person to the intervention counselor, who shows the C.D. person a prearranged seat.

As the escort takes a seat, he or she closes the circle, thus psychologically bringing the C.D. person into the group and symbolically but not physically blocking his exit. The C.D. person looks surprised and usually snaps an angry comment such as, "What's this all about?" The lead intervention counselor responds with a preamble sounding something like this: "Hello, Charlie (or Shirley or whoever). My name is John O'Neill. This is my associate (if there is one). We work with families, and your family and friends came to us a while back because they were concerned about things that were happening in their lives that involve you. Our suggestion was to write down those concerns on a piece of paper so they can express them precisely and with love. They've done that, and so I'd like to ask that you listen to what they have to say. Then you can respond however you see fit. Would you be willing to listen to what they have to say?"

In the vast majority of cases the C.D. person agrees to listen, although sometimes with some snide remark for good measure. The counselor then points to the first intervener, who loudly, clearly, sincerely, and with feeling reads all of his or her statements. Anger is discouraged at the intervention. It should be temporarily put on hold to be dealt with later in treatment. But expressing all other feelings is strongly encouraged. There appears to be a correlation between the amount of tears shed and the impact of the statements. If the C.D. person starts to argue, the intervener stops reading. It takes two to argue, so everyone just remains silent. When the C.D. person quiets down, the intervener continues. One by one, each person reads all of his or her statements. In some cases, the C.D. person has argued with the first few statements, but realizing no one was willing to fight, sat back and listened. Occasionally, a C.D. person has tried to confront others in the group about their own drinking or drugging. We quickly reemphasized that the purpose of the gathering was to share concerns about him, the chemical use of others could be discussed at another time. Sooner or later one of the statements really hits hard emotionally. Perhaps it described a serious event during a blackout or an act that grossly violated his values. The statements of young children in particular often have a very powerful impact. Unless the C.D. person has lost the capacity to feel, this specific but nonjudgmental data will begin to evoke an emotional response. At first it may take a trained observer to discern the impact; a change in breathing rate, downward eye movements, dry-throated swallowing, but often these minimal reactions will build into tears and even sobbing. It is important not to rescue the C.D. person from his pain at this critical moment. Grant him the privilege of, at least on this occasion, paying the emotional price for his drinking or other drugging behavior. It is this pain that fuels the willingness to accept help, so let it work.

When all the participants have presented their statements, the intervention counselor will probably allow a brief period of silence to let the power of the moment run its course. Then he or she will close with a statement such as this: "(Name of C.D. person), your family and friends believe that none of the things they have told you about would have ever happened had it not been for alcohol (or other drugs). They have cared enough about you to learn more about how this chemical affects individuals and families. They know now that some people are so constituted genetically that, if they experiment very long with mood-altering chemicals, episodes of loss of control—such as have been described here—will occur. They also know now that this loss of control happened not because they were bad, stupid, or crazy but because they have an illness. Part of this illness is that those who have it can't see that they've got it. That's why they held this meeting—to tell you as lovingly as possible just how serious your situation has become and how much pain it is causing you and those who love you. They wanted you to see what they have seen. They have found a program here in town (or wherever) that treats this illness and have made reservations for you to enter that program. Would you accept that help?"

Where Do We Go From Here?

From here the intervention can go in several directions. In over half of those that we have facilitated, the C.D. person's response was a variation of "I had no idea things were so bad, that I was hurting so many people so much, and really didn't believe anybody still cared. What do you want me to do?" It is noteworthy that in most of these cases, the family of the C.D. person had predicted that the C.D. person would be angry and negative and refuse help. Many C.D. persons, of course, do not immediately leap at the opportunity for help. Very often the denial will still be extreme and quite vocal. That is why it is important to retain a counselor with the courage, maturity, and skills needed to deal with any emotional barrage from the C.D. person—be it anger, tears, or fears—and then calmly, one by one, put to rest the C.D. person's objections and arguments.

What If He Says No?

During the course of intervention training, the concerned persons will be asked to ponder the question: "What will you do if the C.D. person says no? Will you continue to enable as you have in the past? Are you going to seek or continue to participate in help for yourself? Are you going to set any limits as to how much, if any, drinking- or drugging-related behavior you will accept? Will a "no" affect your future dealings about sex, driving, socializing, or even the continuance of your relationship to him as parent, child, spouse, boss, friend, or neighbor?"

Each participant is asked to be prepared to "recontract" his relationship with the C.D. person if he turns down the offer of help. This step has seldom been necessary in our intervention work. But it has been a very important step for the concerned persons in order to remove the fear of a negative response. At the same time, this "recontracting" requirement helps the concerned persons become more aware of ways in which they are enabling and identifies behaviors they will no longer tolerate. The content of the recontracting statement must be based on what you honestly will or will not do. The counselor can suggest options, but only you can decide. Avoid empty threats. You have probably been threatening throughout this disease and taken no follow-up action. As a consequence, you may have become unbelievable. Now is the time to say what you mean and mean what you say. Here are some examples:

"Mom, Dad says I don't have to ride in the car with you from school when you've been drinking. I'll have my teacher call a cab for me. And if she asks why, I'll tell her the truth."

"Son, if you can't find it in your heart to accept the help offered, I want you to move out of the house before this weekend. There will be no more money. You are on your own. Remember we love you and the help is always there."

"Honey, I'm sorry you won't go to treatment. I intend to get the help that I need to recover from the way your disease has harmed me. From now on I will not call the boss and make excuses for you. If you don't do the chores around the house, they will be left undone. And I insist that there be no physical contact between us when you are under the influence."

"Since you will not accept help, I am leaving with the children and filing for divorce."

Remember, these recontracting statements will rarely if ever have to be employed. But it is important that each participant answer for himself or herself this question: "What will I do if he says no?"

Family Power or Professional Skill?

Most of the interventions we have facilitated required a good deal of adroitly managed dialogue between us and the C.D. person to finally gain his willingness to accept treatment. The skill here is for the counselor to convert the C.D. person's objections and denials into questions to be answered or issues to be discussed rather than differences to be argued about. Under such circumstances, it may seem that the counselor "talked" the C.D. person into treatment. Such is not exactly the case. What does happen is that the emotion-charged presentation of the concerned group's statements and the outpouring of love create an atmosphere in which such persuasions become possible. This mix of concerned-person power and counselor skills merges into the magic that makes this kind of intervention so often successful.

Will It Work?

Emphatically yes! The odds are favorably high provided proven methods are followed. If your counselor is competent, if all the significant others in the C.D. person's life participate, if each of them is properly trained and prepared, if the statements they present are specific and powerful yet packaged in love and concern, and if the help options offered can be accepted with dignity, then there is more than an 80 percent probability that the C.D. person will agree to the help suggested. More importantly, when the above conditions are present, the system of family, friends, and co-workers surrounding the C.D. person has changed in many positive ways. The C.D. person will have to make changes to fit into this healthier system. This is another reason for saying that intervention is a process and not an event. The C.D. person may refuse help in the immediate moment of the intervention. But if those who love him have gotten help for their own co-dependency, broken the no-talk rules, and stopped the enabling, then the process keeps pressuring the C.D. person to see what's really happening and eventually opt for help.

The "What If" Commitment

Not to be confused with the "what if" concerns discussed earlier, the "what if" commitment is a last-ditch effort to achieve some positive results when the C.D. person adamantly refuses treatment. The C.D. person may take the position that "Yes, there is a problem, but I can handle it—I'll quit drinking/drugging on my own (or with the help of A.A., N.A., or other self-help programs)." The intervention counselor will, of course, try to show him how difficult it is to quit without help and even may advise against withdrawal from alcohol or other drugs without close medical supervision. But when every effort to coax the C.D. person into accepting treatment fails and it seems fruitless to go on, the counselor will close out the proceedings by saying something like the following: "I know you mean what you say about quitting (or cutting back), but most people who have experienced the kind of consequences of their drinking/drugging that have been described here find it impossible to return to controlled use or to quit without help." To which the C.D. person will predictably reply, "Well, I know that I can!" At which time the counselor will counter with, "What if you can't? Would you then accept treatment?" The idea is to get the C.D. person to agree that, if he cannot quit on his own, he will immediately enter treatment. Because the C.D. person is so sure that he can stop, he will usually agree. The counselor will then attempt to reinforce and elevate the strength of the commitment: "So you are making this commitment to your family and friends—that if you return to (or can't control) your drinking/drugging, you give your solemn word to immediately enter treatment. Is that correct?" The idea here is to effect another intervention in advance. If the C.D. person does experience further problems—and without a recovery program they just about always do—those who participated in the intervention remind him of his promise and hold him to it.

When the Attempt Fails

Sometimes there is not a happy ending. Usually when the C.D. person's feeling life, or affect as the psychologists call it, is shut down. Touching the pain is what powers the concerned-person intervention. When he can't get in touch with his own pain or the pain suffered by others, what is said has little impact. We recall the case of a five-year-old in tears climbing onto the lap of her father and begging him to "go get well at the hospital" and receiving not a twinge of emotional response. Even when such letdowns occur, it's not the end of the world. Whatever happens it is certainly the beginning of a new life. No more no-talk rules or pretending everything is alright or accepting the unacceptable. You're getting the help to recover, whatever the C.D. person chooses to do. And it isn't over. This is a process and not just a single event. The forces set loose at the intervention will continue to put pressure on the C.D. person to accept help. The ball is now in his court to stay. Even when intervention doesn't work—it sticks...it keeps working.

Loose Ends

Although chemical dependency is a universal disease, it unfolds uniquely in each victim's family. So, too, each intervention will have its own special challenges that may demand innovation and improvisation to overcome. In addition to the two more common outcomes just described, there are infinite variations: the C.D. person might agree to go if someone else in the group who also has a problem will enter treatment as well. (That happened to us once.) Some of the supposed "concerned persons" may turn out to be selling drugs to the C.D. person. (That has happened a couple of times.) The C.D. person whom everyone described as a pussycat will become violently angry, while another, thought to be awesomely threatening, will break down in tears and leap for the help offered. (Those kinds of unexpected reactions happen frequently.) One of the interveners who never shows emotion will break down, and this will have a profoundly penetrating effect on the C.D. person's delusion. (This is also a frequent occurrence, usually involving either a very tough guy or a child who never felt safe enough before to really speak of his or her pain.) C.D. persons have interrupted part way through the gathering and agreed to accept help. Others have refused vigorously, become very angry, and stayed that way for several days following, spouting all manner of windy threats, and then quietly entered the recommended treatment center unassisted.

In summary, the concerned group intervention process is highly effective when the group is properly educated and prepared and the counselor is experienced and skilled. Each effort is unique and exciting with potential for both failure and joy. But none of them we have observed has ever failed to produce more positive results than negative consequences. At the very least, the intervention experience gives the concerned persons a taste of wellness and from that there is no turning back.

Intervening on Other Problems

We are frequently asked about the use of the concerned group approach for other kinds of problems, such as overeating, compulsive gambling, or workaholism. Our knowledge and experience is with chemical dependency. We do know of cases, however, where this approach has been employed successfully to motivate into help those suffering from other kinds of compulsive behaviors. Our suggestion in these cases would be to get professional assistance from someone who has experience using this type of intervention and who also possesses a background in dealing with the particular problem involved.

Follow-Through

There are some steps that should be taken after an intervention attempt to be certain no unfinished business remains. First, if the attempt is successful, the written intervention statements should be saved for possible use in treatment. Either the intervention counselor or one of the interveners should collect them, have the authors write on them that they give permission for the statements to be read again during the treatment process, and inform the treatment center intake staff that an intervention did take place and that the statements were preserved. The data contained therein can be very useful if the C.D. person remains in a state of heavy denial after program entry, a not-uncommon occurrence. Secondly, the concerned persons should gather with the counselor for a "de-briefing." In this meeting participants are encouraged to discuss any questions about upcoming family treatment or any issues left over from the intervention. This is also a chance to process any unresolved feelings experienced as a result of their involvement: fear; anger toward the C.D. person, the counselor, or other participants; joy, relief, or the freedom to feel out loud and reestablish emotional equilibrium. Thirdly, each concerned person needs to recommit to pursue his or her own recovery from co-dependency regardless of the treatment outcome of the C.D. person. And, finally, we recommend that participants take especially good care of themselves physically for a few days following the intervention. This is a very emotionally and physically draining endeavor. It's a good idea to be kind to yourselves—after all, you deserve it. You may have just saved someone's life.

It Always Makes Things Better

Absolute statements—"always," "never," "without a doubt," "every," etc.—are words and phrases that can be argumentative and polarizing. This is especially true when discussing problems as emotion-packed as chemical dependency and co-dependency. So it is with some forethought that we head this paragraph "It Always Makes Things Better." Yet properly conducted intervention preparation is a process that usually stops the enabling, gets some of the concerned persons into help for their co-dependency, and moves family dynamics in a positive direction. This means that, even if the C.D. person initially refuses help, the system in which it was O.K. for him to drink, drug, and behave in inappropriate ways no longer exists. Thus, intervention *always* makes things better, even if the C.D. reacts negatively. There is another important dynamic operating as well. As shown earlier in the discussion of co-dependency, when someone in a family develops a negative condition such as C.D., the rest of the family take on negative survival roles to keep the family system in balance. But this works in the other direction, too. When some of the family members begin to recover from co-dependency, the others—including the C.D. person—must change to accommodate this new wellness. So it is accurate to say that a properly orchestrated intervention effort is *always* successful.

Intervention—A Wrap-Up

Intervention, be it crisis-based, one-on-one, or the concerned group approach, is simply an effort to love the person behind the disease enough to help him see what he is unable to see. All intervention attempts involve concern, specific data, and the offering of help options the C.D. person can accept with dignity. Each type of intervention works best if the statements used are concise, specific, and nonjudgmental. When the interveners are properly trained and prepared, the effort is neither conspiratorial, judgmental, or antagonistic. Rather, it is a genuine act of love, based on well-proven methods and carried out with respect. In some ways, intervention is to chemical dependency as CPR is to cardiovascular disease—an emergency lifesaving procedure but one best conducted by those properly trained and prepared.

Part Three

Understanding
the Problem

9

The Chemical Love Affair

The Deadly Romance

How could someone we love and respect become a slave to alcohol or other drugs? Just as relationships with a C.D. person are a compelling and painful love story, the tales told by victims of chemical dependency are sagas of agonizing love affairs. Recovered C.D. victims universally relate how they were strongly attracted, very early, to the "high" received from mood-altering chemicals. They seemed to quickly develop an especially deep, primitive love relationship with chemically induced euphoria. This special affinity sooner or later led them into orchestrating moods and solving problems with alcohol and drugs *instead of maturing emotionally and refining adult coping skills*. Under those circumstances, alcohol and/or drugs quickly became a "best friend." Other best friends, spouses, children, and co-workers found themselves isolated and even feeling inadequate and guilty because the C.D. person preferred alcohol and drugs to them.

The Eye of the Beholder

Recovered persons describe how alcohol and drugs began to take a paramount role in their lives. They were not *choosing to abuse*. On the contrary, they discovered that they could no longer keep promises to themselves about when, how much, and with what consequences they would drink or drug. It seemed that they had lost the ability to relate to chemically induced euphoria with any predictable consistency. More and more their behavior was influenced by the presence of the chemical. They found themselves doing things they didn't want to do and not doing things they knew they were supposed to do. Loss of control over alcohol and/or other drugs occurred more frequently with more serious consequences. Their loved ones found themselves confused by this behavior, and they too began to feel powerless. Nothing seemed to help, no matter what they tried or how they reacted.

"I'll Take a Double"

C.D. people consistently report developing a tolerance for the chemical very early in their experience. This "hollow leg" phenomenon demanded an increase in dosage—gulping drinks, drinking doubles, drinking before going drinking, mixing booze and pot or booze and pills or cocaine and heroin —in order to continue to reach the same high. Because of this increasing tolerance, the C.D. person remained conscious longer, even though chemical levels in the brain were very high. Behavior under the influence of these high levels often became very bizarre, sometimes grossly violating his values. Family members and friends watched in disbelief and felt more powerless, guilty, and afraid.

They've Changed!

Chemical use at these higher dosages and its associated negative behavior hurt. It caused the C.D. person a great deal of emotional pain—shame, guilt, fear, remorse, self-directed anger, loneliness, and self-hatred. This reservoir of pain grew and began to influence the C.D. person's attitude toward himself, life, and of course those around him. Pain made the world seem a negative place and the people in it very threatening. In order to deal with this pain, the C.D. victim developed an array of defensive behaviors: blame, denial, hostility, aggression, charm, overachievement, withdrawal. These defenses worked temporarily to get people off his back but caused long-term problems in relationships. By now, those who cared about the C.D. person were probably at the receiving end of a great deal of unpredictable and unacceptable behavior. Thus the C.D. person began to drive away those who cared the most. He seemed to have changed into a different person. In fact, what had really taken place is that he had literally *become* his defenses.

And They Lied!

It's still not very acceptable to be a drunk or a drug addict in our society. And most C.D. people know that deep down inside they are good, intelligent, sane people. They couldn't possibly be alcoholics or addicts. After all, folklore had taught them all their lives that persons like themselves don't get that way. As a consequence, they lied to themselves and others to protect their own self-worth. The C.D. persons reported how they minimized, excused, and alibied away their unacceptable drinking and drugging behavior to maintain a level of self-esteem. Either it wasn't as bad as others said, there was a perfectly good explanation, or it would be different next time. This rationalization was simply a knee-jerk psychological reaction on the part of the C.D. persons to protect their own self-image, much in the way people will lie to themselves about baldness, wrinkles, and weight gain. Only the consequences of this self-deceit involved more than vanity; it could have been deadly.

Stuffing

It hurts to mess up, to violate one's own rules of behavior, to break promises to oneself. Yet that is exactly what the C.D. persons said they did over and over in the pursuit of a fatal love affair with chemical euphoria. To escape this emotional pain, the C.D. persons learned to repress unpleasant memories of unacceptable alcohol- and/or drug-related behavior. By quickly stuffing these painful memories in the deeper, less accessible areas of the memory, the C.D. persons were able to escape the shame, guilt, and remorse that closer examination would bring. Unfortunately, this repression deprived the C.D. persons of data that could have helped them see the severity of their condition, and widened the gap between what they remembered versus what those around them actually saw.

Blackouts

As though trying to contribute to this delusion, the chemical itself often caused a form of temporary amnesia called a blackout. In a blackout, the C.D. persons were able to retrieve the memory data necessary to function in the here and now: how to write a check, drive a car, fly an airplane, or even remove a brain tumor. But they temporarily stopped storing long-term memories. There are documented cases of airline pilots not remembering flights and surgeons not recalling operations. Sometimes the blacked-out C.D. persons appeared intoxicated, but on other occasions they may have had enough eyedrops in their eyes, mouthwash on their breath, caffeine in their system, antacids in their stomach, and booze or drugs in their blood to appear and act sober. Yet they were not storing long-term memory data.

One frightening aspect of blackouts is that C.D. persons may not behave in accordance with their values while blacked out. We have seen estimates asserting that over half of the inmates in

United States prisons report not remembering the crime that put them there.

It Was Great!

The irony of the memory breakdowns that deluded the C.D. persons is that, while rationalization, repression, and blackouts prevented them from recalling many drinking- or drugging-related events, they vividly remembered how good they felt. Vernon E. Johnson, founder of the renowned Johnson Institute in Minneapolis, terms this phenomenon "euphoric recall." Apparently human memory of events takes place in the higher, or cognitive, part of our brain, an area that alcohol and drugs tend to inactivate in the early stages of intoxication. But because the deeper-feeling parts of our brain take longer to "short out" by chemicals, the C.D. persons experienced intense recollections of their chemical euphoria. The net result is that they minimized, alibied, excused, twisted, distorted, repressed, and sometimes completely forgot many of their embarrassing behaviors while clearly remembering the euphoria. Meanwhile, friends and family watched in horror and clearly recalled the staggering, word-slurring, emotional abuse, foolhardy risks, insults, or erratic driving that may have actually occurred.

Delusion and Denial

These classic responses of rationalization to protect self-worth, repression to escape emotional consequences, and blackouts causing chemically induced memory losses, and the overriding memory of the euphoric payoff formed a thick wall of delusion surrounding the C.D. persons and blinded them to the impact on themselves and those they loved. This delusion was part of their pathology and the reason few victims spontaneously recover. It may have happened, but you don't often hear of an alcoholic getting up one morning and saying, "I realize I have a problem and have been acting in defensive and bizarre ways, so I think I'll go to an A.A. meeting and get some help." This rarely occurs, because the C.D. person is thoroughly but sincerely deluded.

Put It All Together

That's the story related by one recovered C.D. after another. The circumstances, melodramas and predicaments may vary, but the basic tale can be summarized as follows: A special attraction to the chemical high, followed by a growing tolerance for the chemical, led C.D.-prone persons to loss of control over its use.

This inability to consistently predict the consequences once they drank or drugged led to repeated incidents of conduct under the influence which violated their own value systems. Such unacceptable conduct, incidentally, may have been passive rather than active—not doing the things expected of them as spouses, children, employees, students, or friends. This kind of behavior caused an increasing level of emotional pain. To ease this pain, the C.D. persons took on an array of defensive behaviors. Because it was not O.K. to get this disease, they lied to themselves in order to shore up their weakening self-worth. Then a series of memory breakdowns and quirks combined to surround the whole process in a seemingly impenetrable wall of delusion. And thus we have, in the words of Vernon Johnson, "a primary, progressive, chronic, and terminal disease." It is primary because it must be treated first before any other problems—legal, marital, financial, health, family, or professional—can be dealt with permanently; progressive because all the symptoms described almost always get worse and seldom get better unless intervened upon from the outside; chronic because there is no specific cure, only the means to arrest it; and, finally, fatal because people die from this malady by the thousands.

How Bad Is It?

Chemical dependency is usually acknowledged to be the nation's number three health problem after heart disease and cancer. But if we consider the number of deaths due to alcohol- and drug-related accidents, suicides, family violence, and crime, the problem becomes even more serious. Then suppose we add the number of death certificates which, out of supposed kindness toward the family, state some other "natural" cause instead of chronic alcoholism or drug addiction. And what about including the cancer deaths related to the heavy smoking associated with alcohol and drug use? And then there is the fact that C.D. people are seldom concerned with physical fitness or nutrition and probably experience an inordinate share of early cardiovascular-related deaths. We could go on, but isn't this enough to suggest that C.D. may, in fact, be the greatest cause of premature death in this country? *This is a fatal disease.*

Beyond Controversy

So we are dealing with life-or-death matters. Far too often this disease has a tragic and unnecessary fatal conclusion. Even when physical death is deferred, spiritual death occurs—in the sense that the victim stops pursuing his true potential and fails to achieve once-important dreams, goals, and aspirations. We therefore suggest that—because the very life of a loved one may be at stake—intellectual controversy or extended dialogue about the causes of this condition is a luxury ill afforded.

The fact is that millions of recovered C.D. people could tell the tale we just related. The vast majority of them were obviously otherwise good, intelligent, sane people. They simply could not relate to alcohol or other drugs in any consistently positive way. When those who loved them found the courage to take the critical actions described earlier in this book, intervention and treatment was usually successful. But when nothing happened "from the outside" to interrupt the progress of the disease, spiritual and often physical death was the result.

The next chapter will cover some of the contemporary thought about why people get hooked on alcohol and drugs in the way just described. Some discussion of causes seems to be a necessary step for those trying to cope with C.D. But, as we ponder the reasons why, it's a good idea to keep in mind that this is not just a behavioral or social problem we are facing—it is an often fatal disease.

10

A Respected Consensus

Through the Information Barrier

What causes some people who use alcohol or other drugs to develop the chemical love affair while others escape? The answer is buried in a mass of clouded, confused, and controversial scientific opinion. And the picture is further muddied by the incredible amount of folklore on the subject. Everyone has an opinion, even though most of the information is out of date and gets in the way of rather than aids recovery. Not only is much of our traditional information inaccurate, but there is a great deal of misunderstanding among professionals about the disease as well.

Controversy about C.D.—its causes and treatment—abounds. Intellectualizing can delay action while accomplishing little. Wanting to understand can be tempting because it is easier and less risky to read, think, and talk about the problem than to do something about it. It is not necessary to be an in-depth expert about C.D. in order to intervene upon it. More than likely you have already discovered that this disease cannot be outsmarted. Nor can you reason with the C.D. person about his condition or educate yourself over its impact. In all kinds of ways, chemical dependency is a disease responding much better to common-sense action than high-blown theories. Consequently, this chapter is near the back of the book and presents only a brief overview of basics about the nature of C.D. Our limited purpose is to provide enough information to counter obsolete ideas, understand the major components of the disease, and recognize quality help. But we encourage you to put minimal energy into trying to figure it out and concentrate on actions leading to recovery.

The Consensus

The research picture is now clear enough to know with certainty which beliefs are helping people recover and which are not. Here is one that works. The official program of the 1987 International Congress for Alcoholism and Drug Abuse Counselors held in London stated as its purpose:

> To underscore the basic truth that alcoholism and other drug addictions are biogenetic medical/physical primary diseases that are diagnosable and highly responsive to treatment delivered by trained multidisciplinary specialists in a primary disease, non-drug, 12-step compatible and abstinence-based recovery treatment program.

Such a statement sums up quite well the present mainstream thinking about C.D.: that it is a diagnosable and treatable disease, pure and simple. Since this gathering is attended by the professionals who treat the disease day in and day out around the world, the statement also endorses just which intervention and treatment approaches are achieving success. Our personal belief is that sometime in the future someone will walk off a stage with a Nobel Prize for proving the above description of C.D. to be scientific fact.

An Official Definition

The following is the current definition of alcoholism as approved by the boards of directors of The National Council on Alcoholism and Drug Dependence (February 3, 1990) and of the American Society of Addiction Medicine (February 25, 1990).

Definition of Alcoholism

Alcoholism is a **primary**, chronic **disease** with genetic, psychosocial, and environmental factors influencing its development and manifestations. **The disease is often progressive and fatal**. It is characterized by continuous or periodic: **impaired control** over drinking, **preoccupation** with the drug alcohol, use of alcohol despite **adverse consequences**, and distortions in thinking, mostly notably **denial**.

- **Primary** refers to the nature of alcoholism as a disease entity in addition to and separate from other pathophysiologic states which may be associated with it. "Primary" suggests that alcoholism, as an addiction, is not a symptom of an underlying disease state.

- **Disease** means an involuntary disability. It represents the sum of the abnormal phenomena displayed by a group of individuals. These phenomena are associated with a specified common set of characteristics by which these individuals differ from the norm, and which places them at a disadvantage.

- Often **progressive** and **fatal** means that the disease persists over time and that physical, emotional, and social changes are often cumulative and may progress as drinking continues. Alcoholism causes premature death through overdose, organic complications involving the brain, liver, heart and many other organs, and by contributing to suicide, homocide, motor vehicle crashes, and other traumatic events.

- **Impaired control** means that the inability to limit alcohol use or to consistently limit on any drinking occasion the duration of the episode, the quantity consumed, and/or the behavorial consequences of drinking.

- **Preoccupation** in association with alcohol use indicates excessive, focused attention given to the drug, its effects, and/or its use. The relative value thus assigned to alcohol by the individual often leads to a diversion of energies away from important life concerns.

- **Adverse consequences** are alcohol-related problems or impairments in such areas as: physical health (e.g., alcohol withdrawal syndromes, liver disease, gastritis, anemia, neurological disorders); psychological, functioning (e.g., impairments in cognition, changes in mood and behavior); interpersonal functioning (e.g., marital problems and child abuse, impaired social relationships); occupational functioning (e.g., scholastic or job problems); and legal, financial, or spiritual problems.

- **Denial** is used not only in the psychoanalytic sense of a single psychological defense mechanism disavowing the significance of events, but more broadly to include a range of psychological maneuvers designed to reduce awareness of the fact that alcohol use is the cause of an individual's problems rather than a solution to those problems. Denial becomes an integral part of the disease and a major obstacle to recovery.

It seems clear that regardless of the ongoing debate, as a practical matter the notion that C.D. is a bona fide disease with a strong genetic component is widely accepted and dominates treatment approaches, insurance coverages, and the laws of the land. *Medical and scientific opinion is not divided on the basic concept that C.D. is a disease process in every sense of the word.* The fact that C.D. is a pathology is no longer questioned by specialists in field or those current in their understanding of the research, although there is continuing research and scientific debate about the specific biochemistry.

Why the Controversy?

Why don't we have clear public consensus on this issue of so much importance to many Americans? There appear to be four major reasons for the continued existence of official confusion, denial, hesitancy, and controversy:

1. Low research priorities

2. The emotional impact of the disease on many of those from whom we might ordinarily expect answers

3. The confusion caused by headline-seeking dissenters

4. The conflicts brought on by our own alcohol and drug experience

Research

Part of this national delusion and conflicting dialogue can be blamed on lack of long-term research. As a nation we spend a billion dollars a year on cancer research and half a billion on heart investigation, both deserving efforts, but only 200 million looking into alcoholism, about the same as dental research. And it is not gum disease that is bloodying our streets and highways. Thus, as in most complex but underresearched diseases, there is no single study at which to point that proves the cause(s) and cure(s) of chemical dependency.

Emotional Impact

The research, prevention, and treatment arena is often charged with emotion because many scientists, physicians, psychologists, politicians, educators, and other such influential persons have been personally impacted by living with a victim of C.D. Consequently, studies of C.D. that support the notion of an inherited disease process sometimes fall not just on deaf ears but on powerful prejudices and ragged emotions as well. Respected researchers have more difficulty getting papers and studies on the subject of chemical dependency published in professional journals than on other health care subjects. This is most likely because chemical dependency is seldom just an academic issue. Very few people receive new information about this disease with scholarly objectivity.

Contrast

Consider this: A few years ago, when physicians, politicians, science writers, and newspaper editors picked up research that posed a then tenuous link between dietary cholesterol and heart disease, they were quick to accept and anxious to spread the news to their patients, constituents, or readers. They responded likewise a little later, when a connection between lack of fiber in the diet and certain cancers was first suspected. As a result, these ideas have become part of our popular medical folklore in less than one generation. This conversion has occurred in spite of the fact that there was, and to some extent still is, controversy about the studies that produced these conclusions. Yet research at least equal in scope and validity that points toward C.D. as a genetically transmitted biochemical disease meets awesome resistance. Why? It's as though each disease had the same size wagonload of scientific proof. Yet, when the wagons are pushed up the hill of public resistance, the C.D. wagon keeps rolling back down.

Invisible Barriers

Part of the reason lies in the fact that at least 25 percent of those physicians, scientists, politicians, writers, and newspaper editors (and we might add computer programmers, bus drivers, bricklayers, mechanics, clerks, etc.) who make official pronouncements or generate new folklore are suffering from the effects of living with a C.D. person. They can no more be objective about C.D. than they could be indifferent to a horse that repeatedly kicks them. So an invisible barrier of pain and prejudice seems to block and distort efforts to gain professional and public acceptance of new information. Add to that the fact that perhaps 85 percent of the C.D. victims are in denial and not advocating for causes and cures, while nearly all of the victims of cancer, AIDS, heart disease, etc., are clamoring for more research.

Headline Seekers

Another element in the confusion about C.D. stems from economics. Dissenters from the mainstream make money. For researchers or writers in the human behavior field, the fastest way to get squeezed between the sports scores and the obituaries is to restate that alcoholism and other chemical dependencies are treatable diseases and that the treatment must be based on total abstinence. But to make minor headlines, just claim to have taught a handful of "alcoholics" how to be social drinkers again. Controversy sells! Certainly the writings of the respected researchers and pioneers in this field do get published. However, adding more proof to an existing precept doesn't make for best sellers. On the other hand, articles based on one or another of these "cures" or controversial notions about C.D. sell, and since authors seldom work in the mainstream of C.D. research or treatment, their theories don't have to pass the scrutiny of informed peers. So these "You too can learn to drink safely" notions fall upon an eager audience.

For just about every chemically dependent person wants to hear that there is an easy cure or, better yet, a way to regain control. And what family member or friend of a C.D. person wouldn't like to believe that all the C.D. person has to do is learn to control his drinking. Or that the right combination of vitamins and exercise will cure the problem. In magazine articles and talk show appearances, professional guests from medicine, psychiatry, psychology, and science who are neither expert nor experienced or respected in the C.D. field will sometimes talk of C.D. as secondary to childhood rearing, depression, schizophrenia, homosexuality, excess heterosexuality, vitamin deficiency, Vietnam battle experiences—and the list goes on and on.

Some talk of alcoholics returning to controlled social drinking by way of behavior modification techniques or of drug addicts responding to treatment by another drug. Others claim success employing techniques tested and discarded years ago as ineffective by the respected treatment programs. Sadly, these behavior modification, nutritional, physical fitness, or other easier, softer remedies contribute to the false assumption that there is a solution for C.D. based on ways other than total abstinence and major life changes. Worse yet, they perpetuate those harmful myths in our society.

All of this flies in the face of what surely must be the largest and most ineffective folk medicine experiment ever conducted: trying to control chemical dependencies by means other than abstinence. Millions have tried it, and it simply doesn't work often enough to be considered as a valid alternative. The whole idea is illogical—trying to control loss of control by controlling it. To the credit of the broadcast industry and the responsible periodicals, we do occasionally hear and read from the real authorities in the intervention and treatment field; respected M.D.'s, clergy, and innovative therapists. Their experience and track records make them worthy of attention in better understanding this disease. But be warned, the confusion caused by come-lately headline seekers and pop psychologists can be disconcerting and, more importantly, can cause delays. Our advice is to trust the veteran treatment professionals who can point to real-life families who have recovered as a result of their work. As the back country Hunter said to his bragging associate, "Show me your coon-skins!"

Why Not Controlled Drinking?

The most frequent excursion of the controversy peddlers is the notion of teaching alcoholics to again be social drinkers. Their argument usually goes something like this: By labeling alcoholism as a disease and making abstinence the only acceptable treatment outcome, the door is closed on efforts to develop therapies aimed at controlled drinking. They then cite controversial studies supposedly proving that at least a small percentage of alcoholics can be taught how to return to normal drinking. Now, the validity of these studies can be argued for days. But doing so misses the point: *Why would society want to consider the ability to drink or drug normally as an important life skill, let alone a desired therapeutic outcome?* There is not a single positive human activity that can be performed better under the influence of mood-altering substances. We've known a couple of authors who insisted they could create only while under the influence. But after treatment they admitted that not only were they as creative now but they also meet their deadlines. There are literally millions of recovered and abstaining C.D. persons whose lives bear testimony to the preferability of a chemical-free lifestyle. They can sing, dance, tell jokes, be creative, make love, act spontaneously, and be happy, joyous, and free without the aid of chemicals.

All mood-alterers are physically toxic and cause the user to temporarily become something other than his authentic self. Alcohol, in particular, has an entrenched role in many of our cultural rituals that we are not trying to challenge. *What we emphatically attack, however, is the idea that there is any legitimate clinical need to attempt to restore mastery of these substances in someone whose life has once been severely disrupted by their use.* If asparagus or sweet potatoes or oysters cause problems in people's lives, they simply quit eating them and go about their business. To our knowledge, the concept of controlled drinking as a treatment outcome for diagnosed alcoholics has never been seriously proposed by any respected professional with extensive experience in the treatment of chemical dependency. So our suggestion is, in your personal war on drugs, stay away from the armchair generals and get your advice from the combat veterans. We are not suggesting canceling the first amendment. But the time-worn advice "Keep it simple and insist on proof" is still valid.

Our Own Experience

A major component in our national reluctance to deal with C.D. as the disease it is stems from our own life experiences with alcohol and drugs. Most of us have experimented with at least alcohol and perhaps other prescribed or even illegal drugs. Many of us even abused those chemicals while at college, in the service, away for the summer, or at other times. We quickly learned that abusing booze and other drugs led to physical, behavioral, and emotional consequences. Normal people will not pay that price for a chemical high, so they modified their use with willpower and reason. Since they could do that, it seemed quite logical that others could as well.

When observing someone who can't control his chemical use, it *seems* that C.D. is a behavioral issue or, at best, secondary to some other problem in the victim's life. These conclusions are simple, logical, and dead wrong. Yet, sadly, some of those who cling to these beliefs are the very professionals who are supposed to be making objective judgments about other people's loss of control. Avoiding professionals with such a belief is crucial when you look for help.

The Dilemma

There is so much prejudice, emotional reaction, and misleading information that chemical dependency will most likely not be universally recognized as a treatable disease until there is not just sufficient but also overwhelming scientific evidence to support that contention. But low national priority, limited budgets, and emotions within the scientific community, combined with the conflicting messages from our own alcohol/drug use, are delaying much needed research and discounting the value of the work already done. For all these reasons our folklore clings, with awesome stubbornness, to the idea that C.D. occurs in people because of underlying lack of willpower, ignorance, or mental illness—in spite of the fact that common sense and experience show otherwise.

Common Sense to the Rescue—Sort of

Common sense, backed by validated experience, can be a useful guide when there is conflicting scientific opinion on a subject. Now that we have given controversy its due, let's see what common sense tempered by the experience of others can tell us about understanding chemical dependency.

Are They Bad? Stupid? Crazy?

To begin with, it can be readily observed that our persistent myths continue to fill prisons, cemeteries, and mental institutions with good, intelligent, sane yet chemically dependent people. As many as 85 percent of those in United States prisons are there for alcohol or other drug-related crimes. A state attorney general recently told us that every person executed in that state since the reinstatement of the death penalty had either been chemically dependent or been raised in a C.D. family. This is not to suggest that the gates of the prisons be opened and all the C.D. people released. In fact, part of the intervention process is convincing C.D. persons that they will be held accountable for their behavior under the influence, and many of these criminals are not chemically dependent but simply chose to abuse alcohol and drugs. What we are suggesting, however, is that the prisons, mental institutions, and cemeteries would be far less crowded if we, as a society, better understood how to prevent, recognize, intervene in, and treat this disease. It is obvious that people don't become chemically dependent because they are bad, because too many good people are afflicted. Look at President Ford's wife, Betty. We've met and talked to her, and she's one of the "goodest" women you'd ever want to meet. Yet she underwent treatment for alcohol and other drug dependency in 1978.

It is likewise clear that C.D. does not strike victims because they are stupid or ignorant. Physicians probably have the highest average I.Q. of any major profession. Their education also makes them very knowledgeable about how drugs affect the body, yet there are an estimated 22,000 alcoholic M.D.'s. It is certainly not because "they don't know better."

Another prevalent but erroneous notion is that C.D. people are just folks who have somehow been knocked off of their psychological horse and are just drinking in order to find the courage to get back in the saddle. Many psychiatrists, psychologists, and social workers practicing today were educated to believe—and still believe—the premise that people become chemically dependent because of some underlying psychiatric or emotional disorder. Such an idea is attractive because it implies that the cause of the drinking or drugging can be found and remedied, permitting a return to normal alcohol and/or other drug use. This persistent myth is appealing but doesn't hold up to the evidence. Most treatment programs administer psychological tests and do a psychiatric evaluation when a patient is admitted. The procedures used are well validated and, if administered to the population at large, will show that 10 to 15 percent of the people walking the streets are suffering from an emotional or psychiatric illness warranting treatment. But when these same tests are given, after detoxification, to those entering treatment for alcoholism or other forms of C.D., about the same percentage test psychologically abnormal, as in the population at large. A review of the current research literature on this subject of "dual diagnosis" or "co-morbidity" produces no consensus. What is generally believed, however, is that C.D. is not caused by underlying mental illness and therefore cannot be cured through the use of medications or therapies specific to such problems. In fact, even when there are secondary psychiatric problems, little can be done to help the mental illness until the primary disease of chemical dependency is arrested.

First Families—No Exception

President Reagan described his father's alcoholic drinking. As mentioned, former First Lady Betty Ford is a happily recovered victim of chemically dependency. Former president Jimmy Carter's brother Billy made headlines with his publicly scandalous alcoholic behavior. Unfortunately, his later recovery received far less publicity. Jacquelyn Kennedy's father and Eleanor Roosevelt's father both apparently drank alcoholically, and the list goes on. It does not seem that any of these First Family members were immoral, stupid, or mentally ill. They just found out in a very publicly visible fashion that their brain chemistry couldn't successfully deal with mood-alterers.

Even the Warriors Fell

Military history from Alexander the Great through Ulysses S. Grant and on into today is resplendent with men of extraordinary bravery, brilliance, and leadership who couldn't hold their liquor and nearly died trying. Look at lists of all-star team rosters, MVPs, hall of famers, literary prize winners, Academy Award winners, Medal of Honor recipients, famous painters and composers, and noted politicians. You will find a noteworthy share of courageous, tough, high-functioning, brilliant, morally sound people totally devastated by this disease. Even baronial American industrial dynasties like the Fords and Firestones have fallen victim as well. It seems that C.D. is a most democratic malady, striking anywhere the right genes have found residence without regard to power, intelligence, talent, wealth, ability, or strength of character.

Facts We Do Know

In spite of research deficiencies, much has been learned to improve our understanding of this malady.

- One study of 200 Harvard University graduates over a forty-five-year period demonstrated that the only common factor in the 13 percent who became alcoholic was a family history of alcoholism.

- Respected studies done in Scandinavia and the United States show that identical twin offspring of alcoholics have similar higher alcoholism rates.

- Adoption studies show that children separated from alcoholic parents and raised in non-alcoholic families retain their three to four times greater probability of becoming alcoholic, while children separated from non-alcoholic parents and raised in alcoholic families demonstrate no greater risk than if they had stayed in the non-alcoholic family.

- Certain ethnic groups like Scandinavians, Irish, and Native Americans have very high alcoholism rates, while others, such as Orientals, Arabs, and Jews, have very low rates. Studies among these high- and low-susceptibility groups imply that changes in the environment have little effect on C.D. rates. For example, when Japanese move from Tokyo to New York City, they don't grow to like or tolerate martinis any better.

- It has also been shown that a high percentage of male offspring of male alcoholics have certain distinctly different brain-wave patterns and may metabolize alcohol differently than normal children—from the very first drink. These same findings have now been found in daughters of alcoholics.

- At present there is a $25 million consortium involving six university research centers investigating the genetics of alcoholism. Tissue samples from 600 alcoholic family members are being analysed in a search for genetic clues. This bodes well for the real possibility of a test for genetic predisposition in the future.

Thus, the research tracks with the common-sense observation that alcoholism runs in certain ethnic groups and concentrates in certain families. All this points to a strong genetic component. Because of these many indications, it is quite true to say that most respected scientists in the C.D. field today believe that a primary contributing cause of C.D. to be an inherited predisposition in some people to interact with alcohol and other mood-alterers differently than "normal" people, and in a way that sooner or later leads to loss of control over the use of those substances. Certainly, this phenomenon has consistently been confirmed in tens and perhaps hundreds of thousands of persons who have been observed in treatment over the years. This "wrong way" of interacting with chemicals seems to lead these "prewired" ones to an instinctual rather than a cognitive relationship with alcohol and other drugs. That is, they seem to connect with the chemical at a deeper and more primitive level in the brain than normal people. Once that deeper connection is made, those prone to chemical dependency are no longer able to control their use of alcohol or other mood-alterers with willpower and reason.

At least five neurotransmitters in the brain are being studied as possible sites of this aberrant brain chemistry interaction with alcohol and other mood-altering chemicals. But whatever the precise locus in the brain may prove to be, the tragic life histories of millions of suffering people over tens of thousands of years support the fact that this loss of control is permanent. Once this condition occurs, the only way C.D. people are able to survive is to abstain from all mood-altering chemicals.

Other Factors

To be sure, this disease does not occur in isolation from social and historical context. Certainly legal advertising and illegal pushing, peer pressures, drug-abusing tendencies in our society, and the increased potency of today's street drugs all contribute to the growing numbers of people suffering from C.D. Nonetheless, the weight of studies, research, statistical data, scientific observation, actual cases, expert opinion, and common sense leaves little doubt that C.D. is a medical/biological dysfunction with a genetic component. It seems clear that some people have a special affinity for the effect of alcohol and other mood-alterers and that this evolves into a pathology—a pathology that meets the classic medical definition of a disease in every way. C.D. has an etiology, a classic list of specific symptoms, a progression, and a treatment. Look at enough cases and you cannot help but be convinced that it is not a moral issue, a condition caused by stupid choices, or the symptom of a psychological problem. *It is a disease.*

Much work is being done to unravel the precise neurochemistry of C.D. Medical treatments such as craving blockers, relapse prevention, and ways to repair organ damage are under development, but with our present state of understanding, the only way to treat this disease is through abstinence and major life changes. Clinical observation and follow-up of thousands of recovering C.D. persons shows that most needed therapeutic help to learn to live happily and productively without alcohol and/or other drugs. Family members are also powerfully affected emotionally and behaviorally by living with a C.D. person; they deserve and require help as well. Coming to believe these realities is fundamental to overcoming this disease in yourself or someone you care about.

11

Alcohol and Other Drugs Today

Good News!

Is your situation part of a worsening national alcohol and drug disaster? The media and the politicians would have us believe that it's chemical warfare out there, with the chemicals winning. Well, they aren't—and that's a fact! Certainly major challenges face the

criminal justice system because of the crime and violence associated with the distribution and selling of illegal drugs. There is
an urgent need to get a research, prevention, and law enforcement
jump on the next round of "wonder drugs" that we didn't get on
crack or cocaine. And it is true that almost half of us admit to
knowing a cocaine addict and that one out of three Americans
reports trying to deal with an alcohol problem in someone they
love. So yes, there is little doubt that drinking and drugging is a
significant national problem or that it's big business—some legal,
some illegal. One beer company alone spends over half a billion
dollars a year promoting its products. Nobody has any idea how
much is spent "marketing" illicit drugs. To be sure, there is plenty
of bad news. Yet there is much good news as well. In fact, now
and then there should be a headline that reads "Alcohol and Drug
Situation Improving" because it is.

Surprise Statistics

Abuse of all categories of drugs has decreased sharply since
the epidemic levels of the 1970s. For example, the number of Americans who used cocaine was down from twelve million in 1985 to
eight million in 1988. And the trend is continuing into the 90s. Current marijuana use among 12- to 17-year-olds is at the lowest level
in ten years. A recent government-sponsored survey of high school
seniors shows a marked change in attitudes toward drug use. Four
out of five seniors are now convinced that frequent marijuana use
poses "great risk". Seven out of ten feel that any cocaine use is
dangerous. Over the last twelve years, consumption of wine in the
United States went up very slightly, but beer has leveled off and
distilled spirits—hard liquor—has gone down 25 percent. That's a
major social change.

For all these reasons there is reason for guarded optimism in
the prevention, intervention, and treatment of alcohol and drug dependencies. There is exciting, breakthrough research being done
that improves our understanding. Powerful new family, workplace,
and community intervention techniques are getting results. Excellent treatment programs and effective counseling are now available
in just about every community. The cost of such care is coming

down. As a consequence, alcoholics and other chemically dependent people are now being intervened upon earlier, being treated more effectively, and achieving long-term sobriety at a higher rate. This success means less pain, grief, and expense for families, friends, employers, the country—all of us. So, on balance, the news is good.

The Stars Are Coming Out

Highly visible spheres of influence such as the armed forces, the professional sports leagues, the motion picture and television industry, and countless companies, large and small, have launched aggressive prevention, intervention, and assistance programs. Betty Ford, Elizabeth Taylor, and the host of other celebrities and athletes who have bravely gone public with their C.D. treatment have softened much of the stigma. Their courageous revelations have given permission and inspired others still suffering to seek help. Just seeing the media reports about these celebrity "coming out parties" has caused many health professionals to rethink their role and update their knowledge and skill. The public now knows that this is a disease that can strike anyone.

A condition many thought only existed in back alleys and under bridges is now being recognized in the country clubs, board rooms, churches, and kitchens of the nation. Because of this destigmatization, more people are reaching out for help sooner. Thus, consumer demand for quality care has put pressure on the health service industry, and it has responded. At the same time, a multitude of self-help groups, spinoffs from the model of the highly respected and long-successful Alcoholics Anonymous program, are providing remarkably effective and absolutely free folk therapy for the whole gamut of addictive/compulsive behaviors. All this is part of a cultural shift away from negative drinking and drugging lifestyles that were once admired but are beginning to be frowned upon. So even though the adverse impact of alcohol and drugs is still significant, it is accurate to say that times are hopeful because use patterns are changing in positive ways and because enlightenment, encouragement, and help for alcohol and other drug problems are all around.

Illegal Drugs Are Scary

In spite of all this good news, when someone we love gets involved in the illegal drug scene, there is often a special sense of fear and bewilderment not experienced when the drug is alcohol. The situation is more frightening perhaps because there are so many unknowns. Alarms are intuitively triggered because you correctly sense that a higher percentage of those who do try these other drugs become addicted. Probably 80 percent of a population could use alcohol all of their lives without becoming alcoholic. Nearly anyone, however, who experiments for very long with the likes of cocaine, heroin, amphetamines, tranquilizers, or their analogs can become pathologically dependent. The research hints that just about everyone has "receptors" in the brain for these kinds of drugs. Thus, a good deal of the confusion about the drug scene derives from the fact that, although far more people use alcohol than all other mood-altering chemicals combined, only a relatively small percentage will become pathologically dependent or alcoholic.

On the other hand, far fewer people are using drugs other than alcohol, but a higher percentage become dependent. Then, too, in the past, except for legally prescribed mood-alterers, it's been tough and expensive to get "drugs." Illegal drugs had to penetrate the borders and defy law enforcement efforts before invading our cities. Or a physician had to be corrupted into writing illegal prescriptions. All those factors restricted availability and added to the risk and cost. But nowadays there are new generations of cheaper, more powerful, and sometimes even temporarily legal "designer" drugs being manufactured in garage and basement laboratories. And inhalant substances such as glue, paint, gasoline, and solvents are available through retail outlets selling them for their intended lawful purposes. For most people this all seems foreign and confusing.

It can be kept simple. If someone you love is messing up his or her life, it really matters little which drug is involved. Whether legal or illegal, drunk, snorted, shot up with a needle, or smoked in a pipe, all these substances wind up in the bloodstream. From there they are carried to the part of the brain that controls feelings, moods, and instincts. When the imprint takes place at a deeper and more primitive level than it does in "normal" people, a dependency develops. If the drug is alcohol, such dependency is called alcoholism. Other drug"isms" develop the same way.

No one yet knows how to reverse the process and enable those who have once lost control to regain it. Abstinence is the only way the alcoholic or otherwise chemically dependent person can keep from pulling the loss-of-control trigger on himself. In addition, once a person crosses the invisible line separating controlled use from the loss of control, there seems to be no turning back, *regardless of the chemical involved.* Literally millions of alcoholics over the centuries have found that they cannot safely use any other mood-alterer, either. The same cross-dependency phenomenon occurs in persons once addicted to cocaine, narcotics, tranquilizers, and so forth. From then on, chemical highs from any substance legal or illegal, including alcohol, seem to trigger loss of control as well.

Although the chemistry and pathology involved in this cross-dependency is still not entirely clear, the real-life consequences are quite obvious. There seems little doubt that, once the primitive brain falls in love with chemically induced euphoria, it can no longer consistently discriminate the source of that feeling. Or as an ex-drunk once said, "The cucumber has crossed an invisible line to picklehood and there is no turning back."

False Alarms

Because there is so much alarm about illegal drug abuse, many of us do tune out until it hits home. The media have emphasized heroin junkies and street gangs roaming the cities, young professionals snorting coke on the job, amphetamine-crazed truck drivers endangering the highways, and the school kids literally going to pot. There are shocking tales of pro ballplayers dropping dead in the prime of their youth, rock stars falling off concert stages in comas, and movie stars trying to bring carry-on bags full of illicit substances through customs. We are warned, at every turn, how this ever-more treacherous drug scene is an awesome threat to our homes, families, and respected ways of life. After a while, it is easy to tune out—to leave the problem to the police, the government, and the other war-on-drugs warriors.

A War Against the Wrong Enemy

The so-called war on drugs is an especially sensitive issue among those who battle this disease on a daily basis through prevention, intervention, and treatment. We certainly believe there is a drug crisis and that extraordinary measures are in order. But most of us, and we believe we can speak here for most in our profession, are convinced that the present goals and priorities miss the mark. Generally, the following criticisms are voiced:

1. Alcohol, the most used, abused, and costly drug, is seldom if ever mentioned in the war on drugs in spite of the fact that three hundred people a day die from alcohol, while five die from crack or cocaine. (Studies have also shown that many death certificates cover up links to alcoholism.)

2. Approximately 80 percent of the drugs are consumed by 20 percent of the users—those who have become dependent. Yet the funding emphasis is on interdiction and law enforcement instead of prevention, intervention, and treatment.

3. Potentially catastrophic realities are being ignored. For example, AIDS is rapidly shifting from a gay disease to an addict disease. (Nearly half of the IV drug users in New York and New Jersey now test HIV-positive.) It costs the health care system $400,000 to treat a terminally ill AIDS patient. That same addict could be intervened upon before he or she got to the needle-using stage and treated at the prestigious Betty Ford Center for less than $12,000. *Yet funding for treatment was cut by two-thirds during the Reagan-Bush-era war on drugs.*

4. Prevention programs continue to emphasize naive concepts, while placing little emphasis on the entry-level drug, alcohol, or helping young people to assess their biogenetic potential for C.D.

5. Research funding priorities are way out of line in relation to the severity of the problem.

Consider This Hypothesis

At any given time over the last three decades the number of persons willing to experiment with illegal drugs has remained relatively constant. An educated estimate would place that potential market at around fifty million people. Each succeeding generation was marketed by their contemporary crop of drug dealers with whatever the wonder drug of the time happened to be. Gradually, as the substance was exposed as toxic, addictive, and often deadly, the experimenters stop using it. So the customer base shrank to the small percentage (perhaps 15 to 20 percent) who had become dependent on that drug and couldn't quit. That's not enough to sustain an "industry," so the dealers moved on to other market niches and offered newer, more glamorous "products." Thus historically there were the hippies of the sixties and seventies with marijuana, the yuppies of the seventies and eighties with cocaine, and now the "yuckies" (young urban crack/cocaine kids) of the eighties and nineties.

Today's war on drugs is more sensational because of the enormous sums of money involved and the violent crime associated with the distribution system. Yet the basic dynamics involved are still the same: As the drug's harmful effects are integrated into street folklore, the experimenters wise up and quit, leaving only the tragic chemically dependent victims as consumers. Thus demand goes down. The accompanying drop in prices combined with modest gains in law enforcement drives the dealers temporarily out of business. And once again it appears that the current war on drugs is over and the good guys won. Then another generation grows into the market niche and from around the corner comes another "harmless, nonaddictive, no-side-effects pleasure potion" complete with new and even more vicious drug lords. And the battle begins anew.

The Numbers

A further look at some numbers may help clarify the order of battle in the war on drugs. As noted earlier, statistics about alcohol and drug use vary widely, are contested by differing factions, and are based on controversial definitions. Nonetheless, a conservative interpretation of the data shows that approximately 90 percent of Americans have tried alcohol, while only about 10 percent report having experimented with other drugs. According to an ABC News poll, 66 percent of those asked admit to frequent alcohol use, while only 4 percent own up to recurring illicit drug use. Now, as we said, those accosted on the street by pollsters inquiring about their illegal drug use might well be less than honest. Still, it's probably fair to say that the drunks far outnumber the dope fiends on Main Street. Perhaps more important is the fact that *at least one hundred and fifty thousand die annually from alcohol-related deaths* versus about four thousand from illicit drugs. There are probably no more than eight million "drug addicts" in the United States, while there may be more than twenty million alcoholics.

Why Focus on Alcohol?

More people use alcohol than other drugs, and more become dependent on alcohol than all other drugs combined. Alcohol causes far more crime and social problems. The damage caused by alcohol in the home, on the street, and in the workplace costs far more than that caused by other drugs. This is essentially true in all age groups, cultural niches, and geographical locations. So alcohol is our number one drug problem. *Alcohol is also the historical and traditional fountainhead of the folklore surrounding all other mood-altering drug use.* Belief that intoxication is a desirable state of affairs is an alcohol-based tradition. The notion that chemically altering your mood improves social intercourse emanates from alcohol history. The concept of relieving stress chemically is an alcohol heritage. The idea that joy and celebration are enhanced by mild—or not so mild—inebriation and all the rituals that go with it is an alcohol myth. And the message that says anybody can drink safely if they just use common sense and good judgment—if they are "responsible drinkers," as one whiskey ad urges—is the greatest alcohol myth of all.

What Can Be Done?

We are not trying to pour out anybody's sippin' whiskey. But the alcohol industry must be convinced, coerced, or, if necessary, sued and legislated into changing its marketing strategies. At present, the industry follows the course of least marketing resistance. It sells to the 20 percent of the drinkers who consume 80 percent of the alcohol. Unfortunately, many of that 20 percent are the suffering alcoholics. The following steps would be a beginning remedy to that situation:

1. Stop all alcohol advertising in places accessible to children. (By the age of eighteen the average kid has seen 100,000 beer commercials on television.)

2. Provide clear warning labels on all products advising users of the potential physical harm and addictive properties of the contents.

3. Subsidize national education programs that warn the public of the precursors and early warning signs of alcoholism.

4. Stop all lobbying activities aimed at preventing passage of stricter laws concerning the public use of alcohol—i.e., drinking at parks, beaches, sports events, and community festivals; while operating vehicles or traveling on airplanes; when gatherings include young people; and so forth.

This would be no more than temporary hardship to the alcohol manufacturers. Unlike the awesome health consequences facing the cigarette industry, many people can safely use alcohol. All the beer and liquor makers have to do to be socially responsible is to refocus their merchandising toward those who can safely use their products, adequately warn those who can't, and stop fighting efforts to protect the public safety. Such actions regarding alcohol use would go a long way toward changing national attitudes about the entire role of mood-alterers. It will no doubt take generations, but we must destroy the myth that properly functioning human minds and emotions can be improved by mood-altering chemicals—that a booze high or other drug-induced high is "better" than natural harmony and serenity—that alcohol-triggered feelings of camaraderie are better than real-life brotherhood and genuine heart-felt love—that celebration is enhanced through sedation...and the insane notion that toxic, addictive, empty-calorie intoxicants are desirable fare for intelligent people.

Back to the War

So yes, there needs to be a war on drugs. But the enemy needs to be more clearly defined and the forces concentrated on the right targets. Education and prevention need to focus on changing national attitudes about the whole idea of intoxication as a positive experience—with appropriate emphasis on Drug Number One: alcohol, and on clear warnings of the disease potential lurking in experimental drug use. Peer-based programs work best. Young people don't listen to experts. They listen to other kids who make sense. Intervention and treatment must be at least as available as the drugs are. That means neighborhood-based programs that speak to the cultural needs of the people they are trying to help. There are many successful models of such programs. They are cheap, effective, easy to start up, and essentially self-sustaining.

Remember the concept: 20 percent of the users consume 80 percent of the drugs, and those users are the ones suffering from C.D. Shift the funding from interdiction and law enforcement to intervention and treatment and you destroy most of the market. *That's how to win the war on drugs cost-effectively.* Finally, the law enforcement effort needs reorganization. The present scattered "war effort" violates the very principles of war. There is no clear mission statement, obvious commander-in-chief, coordinating staff, centralized command and control system, concentration of force, or sustained application of power. It's an overpublicized and under-funded nightmare of an operation unworthy of the first-class organizations tasked to perform its ill-defined and misdirected skirmishes.

A Research-Based War on Drugs

Science is now positioned to provide the answer to the truly age-old questions: "Who is abusing on purpose?" and "Who has a disease of impaired control?"

Research technology breakthroughs now make it likely that science will pinpoint the precise neurochemistry of alcoholism and related addictive diseases in the near future. These breakthroughs will allow clear differentiation between willful alcohol and other drug abuse and pathological alcohol or other drug dependencies.

Researchers already are in agreement about where in the brain the drugs of addiction operate. Science is also convinced that genetics play a significant role in determining who will become addicted. The genetic, neurochemical and biological research technologies and skills needed to probe and explore the mechanisms of alcoholism and other drug dependencies are now available. Exploiting those medical research developments can lead to objective medical diagnostic tests, discovery of genetic markers for addictive disease, non-addictive specific relapse prevention medicines, and even direct medical treatments to intervene and arrest the disease. As this unfolds, we can expect more and more involvement by mainstream medicine in the intervention and treatment of addictive diseases.

As a consequence of this "medicalization" of addictive disease treatment, the alcohol and related diseases should be considered as bona fide *medical* pathologies in the conceptualization of any national health care system, and medical research into basic causes and more specific treatments should have a high priority.

There is no doubt that addictions are a major public health challenge. Researchers are providing mounting evidence that today's psychosocial treatment modes work well enough to more than justify their costs. Even without the treatment breakthroughs described here, it is clear that treating addictions early saves the larger cost—cirrhosis, heart disease, cancer, or AIDS—that often result from untreated addictions.

Raising the priority for research to the same level as law enforcement, prevention, and treatment promises new approaches that can bring about enormous savings in health care, criminal justice, and social programs. These payoffs, combined with the increased national productivity to be gained, present a cost-to-benefit ratio rarely seen in the public policy arena.

There is no greater health care bargain than today's alcoholism and related disease treatment, and no more promising opportunity for dramatic savings in lives, property, and tax dollars than to support a major, research-based war to end the addiction epidemic.

Summary

There is many a battle yet to be fought, but the defense in the war on drugs is catching up with the offense. There is strong positive change moving across our land. The message is getting around that drugs are out and reality is in. Truly enlightened changes in government policies, personal lifestyles, and individual attitudes about alcohol and drug use are rounding the corner into full view. For all these reasons we believe that alcohol and drugs in America are matters of major concern but should rightfully be seen through a hopeful framework.

On balance, the picture can be summed up as follows: Alcohol and other legal and illegal drug abuse and dependency are very serious national problems, but the threat is not growing at the rate the headlines would seem to indicate. With strong central leadership, clear guidelines, and concentration of force, the war on drugs can be won.

Alcohol is still by far the most widespread and damaging drug of abuse, but a higher percentage of those who use drugs other than alcohol become dependent. These alcohol or other drug dependencies are observed to have specific genetic, biological, and psychological components, and have been defined as a treatable disease called chemical dependency. These C.D. persons constitute the primary market for alcohol and other drugs. Therefore, the major focus of the war on drugs needs to be on the prevention or early intervention and treatment of these victims. This and research to find real causes and true remedies is far less expensive than waiting for the disease to progress and paying the cost of crime, violence, imprisonment, welfare families, AIDS, etc.

When somebody you care about becomes a victim of C.D., the situation can be confusing and painful. Yet there is no justification for panic, but lots of reasons for hope, both as a nation facing a serious health and social problem and as individuals confronting an alcohol or other drug problem in someone we love. In today's more enlightened climate, there is effective, professional, and affordable help out there. It is possible, through intervention and treatment, to get the C.D. person to accept recovery as a logical, attractive, lofty choice. Treatment brings an array of positive pay-offs into the lives of C.D. persons and their families. What all this means to you is that it will be easier to deal with a loved one's problem in an era where intoxication is more frowned upon, drugs are no longer "in," and quality help is all around.

Part Four

Finding the Resources

12

When You Can't Afford Help

The Money Issue

Quality in counseling and treatment, like quality elsewhere, costs money. Concern about the financing of recovery tends to reduce itself to four key questions: Are professional chemical and co-dependency treatment programs really necessary? Are they worth the price? Can you afford them? What if there is little money and limited or no insurance?

Is This Really Necessary?

We think the answer is yes. The debate usually centers around the efficacy of A.A. and other twelve-step programs versus formal treatment. Yet if you observe the recovery scene for decades, as we have, it is evident that there is no conflict between the two approaches. Each plays an important role, and they mutually reenforce each other. The ideal is to integrate both and derive the synergistic effect that results. As described earlier, this essentially biogenetic disease begins with powerlessness over alcohol and other mood-altering chemicals. But with this powerlessness unfolds an awesomely complex array of symptoms: physical illnesses, emotional problems, legal entanglements, marital strife, financial messes, sexual dysfunctions, troubled children, workplace frictions, damaged self-esteem, family communication breakdowns, and more. It is simply impossible to confront all these issues clearly and deal with them in a timely and lasting manner without special therapies conducted in a therapeutic atmosphere.

You can conquer the powerlessness with the help of a twelve-step program and then peck away at these secondary problems with self-help efforts, occasional individual counseling sessions, and years of "working on your program." But there is no real substitute for the Big Three: an intensive and structured treatment experience, professionally facilitated aftercare, and sustained lifetime participation in a twelve-step program. That's the best of all possible combinations.

People do achieve a measure of recovery without special assistance. A.A. and the other twelve-step programs have proven eminently successful in helping chemically dependent and co-dependent people overcome compulsions, clear away the wreckage of the past, and raise the victim's life to a higher spiritual plane. It is for these results that involvement in a twelve-step program is recognized as a core element in just about all respected treatment programs. But twelve-step programs are not designed to aggressively batter down and eliminate vestiges of delusion and denial;

screen for medical and psychological symptoms; aggressively confront defensive behaviors; dig into and process deeply buried emotional pain; sort out and mend the aftermath of painful family issues; provide current education about the disease; counsel regarding sexual dysfunctions, smoking, weight control, nutrition, and finances; offer physical and/or occupational rehabilitation; or teach specific skills for adult living such as communication, assertiveness, relaxation, and grieving. First-rate treatment centers address all those aspects of the disease and more.

On the other hand, those who just undergo treatment but forgo twelve-step involvement afterward seem to have a higher relapse rate. So is twelve-step program involvement necessary to recovery? Absolutely! if you want quality recovery and the odds against relapse on your side. Is treatment necessary? Positively! if you want to deal with all the issues and all the pain. It is enlightening to attend a twelve-step group meeting and observe the quality of recovery in those who have experienced treatment and those who have not. There are certainly notable exceptions, but for the most part the untreated will be viewed as successfully dealing with the pain, while the treated have successfully put most of it behind them. Both are success stories, but, as you will observe, all success is not equal. Treatment does pay off. It is worth the cost.

Is the Price Fair?

Even in this era of frightening increases in medical costs, the price of C.D.-related treatment has consistently been decreasing. There are three main reasons: First, experience has shown that unless the patient lacks a work or family support system or is suffering from serious medical or psychiatric problems, treatment may not need to be conducted in expensive hospital-based inpatient facilities. The trend has been toward less costly nonmedical and, wherever possible, outpatient settings. Second, because of increased awareness about intervention, C.D. victims are accepting help at earlier stages of the disease when treatment seems to be more effective. And third, competition is driving cost down almost everywhere. The medical director of one national treatment organization recently told us that in one region of the country they had been forced to reduce their fees by nearly two-thirds to meet the competition. The marketplace offers a variety of C.D. and co-dependency programs—which makes the cost highly competitive. So shop carefully, and you will pay only a fair price for quality treatment.

Will My Insurance Pay?

God only knows! In this era of managed care, HMOs, Medicare, and state and federal regulations or lack thereof, insurance coverage for chemical and co-dependency treatment is a very cloudy picture. In our state, for example, a few years ago the insurance authority ruled that health insurance companies *must* offer its client organizations coverage for alcoholism and other chemical dependencies. The intent was to encourage universal payment for these illnesses in order to motivate more victims to seek early help. (A number of studies had shown that in the long run this saves insurance costs: it's cheaper to treat early alcoholism now than terminal secondary illnesses later.) Up until that ruling, most insurance companies in the state had been paying for C.D. treatment under the nonspecific category of mental or nervous disorders. But after the new ruling went into effect, many organizations, *including many state government agencies*, when offered the specific coverage, refused it. During this same confusing era, some federal government agencies, for a period of time, stopped offering to their employees most coverage for these diseases. These particular glitches have been remedied now.

On the other hand, the Supreme Court once ruled that the Veterans Administration could deny benefit extensions to C.D. veterans. So there seem to be cycles of enlightenment, then retrenchment, regarding insurance coverage. Thus, third-party payment is often a confusing picture. Certain health insurance policies specify alcoholism and related disease benefits, while others clearly exclude or limit coverage. Some providers make no mention of these maladies, yet in fact pay for most treatment costs. As a general rule, the majority of health insurance programs will pay 80 percent of the fees charged by properly credentialed treatment facilities. Yet so-called managed care often brokers treatment choices based on cost reduction rather than appropriate patient-treatment matching.

Coverage seems to go through these confusing cycles, so we recommend taking your policy in hand and visiting the admissions office of a local treatment center. Ask them to check out the coverage. They will be pleased to do so since they would like to get your future business.

HMOs

There are many outstanding health maintenance organizations (HMOs) providing quality medical care at an attractive cost. We have, however, encountered some HMOs that do not have trained C.D. and co-dependency specialists on their staffs. Consequently, C.D. members or their families stand a good chance of falling into the traps described in Chapter 3. If you belong to one of these organizations, you may want to check out the help it offers for alcoholism or other drug dependencies. And find out if there is any provision for counseling/treatment of co-dependency. Should the program be found lacking, you may want to switch to another form of health care protection before seeking help. Otherwise there is the potential for getting inappropriate or ineffective remedies from the HMO while at the same time establishing a preexisting condition that could prevent reimbursement—at least for a waiting period—from any subsequent coverage you might acquire.

What About Special Programs?

As C.D. treatment has developed, it has become clear that certain populations do better in programs designed to meet their special needs. Certainly adolescents need treatment separate from adults. Gays and lesbians seem to do best in treatment programs specifically designed for homosexuals. Women-only programs or those offering special tracks for females claim greater recovery rates. Special issues pertinent to these select populations can best be addressed in the safety of others experiencing those same problems. One powerful example of these needs stems from the shockingly high rate of sexual abuse in chemically dependent women. That subject is better dealt with in a program sensitive to that issue.

There are many so-called Impaired Professional Programs aimed at M.D.'s, attorneys, dentists, pharmacists, veterinarians, nurses, etc. A number of these centers have outstanding treatment models, highly trained staffs, and hard-earned national reputations. Some, however, simply use the impaired professional aegis as a marketing ploy.

If you are considering such a choice, check out the reputation of the facility with the appropriate professional organization (Medical Society, Dental Association, Bar Association, etc.).

There are arguments for and against special programs. One side says "Don't make the C.D. professional special. Their ego is already in the way of recovery." Others make the case that physicians, attorneys, and other professionals do have unique challenges to recovery and deserve and require customized mized approaches. Our experience shows that physicians, clergy, and attorneys do better in programs tailored to the sensitivities of those vocations. Most M.D., clergy, or lawyer treatment models involve longer-term in-patient care and more closely supervised aftercare. Those approaches seem to pay off in higher quality recovery. As for other C.D. professionals, we suggest taking advice of recovered C.D. people from that particular career. Again, consult with the appropriate professional association for advice.

We Can't Afford It!

Frequently, suffering family members lament: "This intervention and treatment sounds great, but we don't have that kind of money and there is no insurance." The choices may be difficult, but the cost of intervention and treatment must be weighed against the penalties for delay. Economic disaster goes hand in hand with chemical dependency. D.W.I. fines and legal fees; auto accidents; lawsuits; divorces; illness and injury; job loss or damage to professional credentials and reputation; money wasted on booze, drugs, and associated carousing; gambling; and poor business decisions can produce a terrible dollar toll. In a year and half or so the typical alcoholic can spend as much on booze as the cost of treatment. And we've encountered cocaine users who snort away that much in a month. So, compared with the expense of allowing the disease to continue, treatment is a very cost-effective choice. This may mean selling the family jewels, giving up the annual vacation trip, or going into debt. It's still probably worth it. For without help, the resources of a C.D. family dwindle away with the progress of the disease. The corny old salesman's adage applies in a very real sense. "You can't afford not to buy treatment."

But If You Truly Can't Afford It

Suppose help is honestly beyond financial reach. There are still options. It may take a bit of street-smarts and some hard work, but it is possible to accomplish all the help actions we've written about by using low-cost or no-cost-to-you resources. Consider this analogy: People with lots of money can go to a single department or grocery store and buy everything they need in one stop—within reason—without regard for price. Not being similarly blessed financially, you may find it necessary to watch for sales, clip coupons, buy different products at different stores to get the best values, and just generally put more energy and shrewdness into your clothing or grocery shopping. Using the same approach, it's possible to fill your recovery bag with all the needed services. Here are some ideas:

- Try to negotiate affordable fees. Some helping professionals and treatment centers charge sliding-scale fees based on ability to pay.

- Check with the best counselors and programs to see whether you can make some kind of payment arrangement. A facility with empty beds to fill may consider some kind of extremely long-term payment plan. Some health care organizations today even accept credit cards.

- Ask local private treatment centers if they have any free or reduced-cost bed spaces allocated for those in need.

And be sure to take advantage of the many free services available in your area:

- The local Council on Alcoholism and Drug Abuse may offer free information programs on alcohol, other drugs, and on intervention for families. This local council may even provide no-cost intervention counseling. They sometimes offer out-patient treatment as well. If not, the council can probably steer you to a treatment center that presents low-cost or no-cost community information programs and intervention assistance.

- Investigate tax- or donation-supported programs for which your family may quality (V.A., state hospital, fraternal organizations, local mental health agencies, etc.). Many of these programs are excellent and employ some of the most competent and dedicated professionals in the field.

- Call the United Way office and ask for the names of any C.D.-related services funded by the agency.

- Contact your community Council of Churches and see whether there may be members of the clergy in your town who are trained in intervention and C.D. counseling.

- Join a self-help program like A.A., Al-anon, Alateen, Narcotics Anonymous, Co-Dependents Anonymous, or Adult Children of Alcoholics. They are nearly always available, and there are no dues or fees for membership. The people you meet there will help you find additional affordable help.

- Go to the library and browse through the many excellent books on alcoholism and other drug problems. The librarian can help you locate them.

- Write the state alcoholism authority. Your local council on alcoholism and drug abuse can provide the address. There may even be a local office. This state authority is responsible for channeling millions of dollars in state and federal aid into education, research, and direct care. Ask them for help.

- Consult the list of resources in the back of this book for additional leads that may be helpful.

The point is, don't give up. You may be poor or perhaps just temporarily broke, but you are not without imagination and common sense. So put to work the same savvy and resourcefulness that you use when shopping for food and clothing and services. Shop around until you pull together the resources needed to help your family. Keep in mind the hopeful fact that the helping community in the field of chemical dependency is replete with those who have also suffered from this disease. Though they may be "professionals" who make their living assisting others, most of them won't let you down just because you're broke. If you reach out, somehow, someway, someone will take your hand.

13

Finding Courage and Support

The News Is Good

In this book we've tried to restore hope, give useful perspectives, and suggest proven paths and guidelines. Chemical dependencies are awful things, and living with a victim is a most disturbing experience. But the trends are positive. National awareness abounds.

Use and abuse seems to be leveling off. Getting high is no longer an "in" thing to do. With less and less cultural tolerance of intoxicated behavior, the victims of C.D. are beginning to stand out. That means earlier intervention and therefore less damage to victims and families. More professionally based help is available. Competition for the treatment of this "new" disease is lowering the cost of care. Realization by the insurance industry of the cost benefits derived from providing better coverage for these illnesses is helping families to pay for quality treatment. The challenge of managed care is resolving itself through better cooperation and communications between providers and insurers. Organizations such as the National Treatment Consortium are taking the actions needed to bring together employers, insurers, and treatment providers.

Practical early intervention methods have proven very effective. Recent excellent, well-validated studies show that treatment does bring about full recovery in most cases. And an impressive array of community-based help resources and self-help programs is available just about everywhere. So there is every reason to feel positive and be hopeful. On balance the news is good. The help is out there and it does work.

Afraid and Alone

The apparent hopelessness of chemical dependency and co-dependency steals away the todays of our lives. Because the present is so painful, thoughts and energies project into the future with fear and anxiety or dwell on the past with guilt and remorse. Yet, in order to take positive steps with these diseases, it is vital to operate in the here and now—where choices can be made that will lead to wellness. Making those choices takes courage and support. C.D. families give up their power of choice as they learn how to survive in an atmosphere of fear and isolation. Survival may ease the pain temporarily, but it is not recovery. To really break free from this trap takes choices. And to make those choices you will need new sources of courage and support.

There is a modern-day fable about a big-city policeman who encountered a sad-faced alcoholic on a shadowy street corner. The pitiful man was on his knees, slowly circling a lamppost. His frightened face was just inches away from the post, and he was beating on it with both fists. Over and over he cried, "Help me! Please help me!" The policeman tapped him gently on the shoulder with his club and asked, "What's wrong?" "I'm walled in," was the pathetic reply. Such is the feeling that paralyzes the C.D. family—a sense of hopelessness, powerlessness, and isolation. Yet, just as with the sad fellow in the fable, all that's needed is to turn outward to find sources of courage and support.

The First Stop

Carl Jung, the revered pioneer of modern psychiatry, once said that after midlife all problems are fundamentally spiritual. He might well have made the same observation about chemical dependency and co-dependency. Recovery from these maladies is essentially a spiritual task. Keep in mind here that spirituality is not necessarily "religionality," although many do find a formal religion to be the most accessible path to a spiritual dimension in their lives. However, for many others, the experience of living in a C.D. situation has brought spiritual despair. It is toward them, in particular, that these next few words about spirituality are aimed.

By spirituality we mean tuning into and connecting with the power sources that reside in the universe outside ourselves—nature, other people, the collective wisdom of the ages, and the love, truth, justice, and beauty that surround us. Some choose to call that power God. What to call this "power greater than ourselves" is optional. The fact that we need such power to recover isn't optional. Communion with this sense of beingness may translate into a belief in a personal, good, and loving God— and it may not. But however we may choose to connect, connect we must. We live in a little box of space and time and possess only limited control over even that small domain. Yet there is a whole universe of circumstances and events that make up our lives over which we have no apparent control. We must either see this larger domain as chaos rushing toward nothingness or as an elegant mystery gradually revealing its rhyme and reason. Opting for chaos dooms us to a life of despair, self-pity, and, worst of all, inaction. The ultimate symptom of C.D. and co-dependency is spiritual darkness. Recovery from these diseases demands the light of faith in the fundamental goodness and order of the visible world, an abiding acceptance of the notion that pain is not the way things are supposed to be, that suffering is an aberration, and that not actualizing into the person you were meant to be is—beyond all else—unnatural.

Transcendence

What has happened to the victims of these diseases is that they have stopped becoming what they were meant to be. Recovery from chemical dependency and co-dependency means getting back on schedule and on course toward becoming our very best possible selves. This means more than just breaking addictions or modifying behavior. It is coming to believe that our role in this universe is to grow into the unique creatures we were meant to be. Achieving such rebirth and renewal requires more than simply repairing the separate broken parts of us. There isn't enough time in a human life to fix piece by piece all of the emotional, behavioral, financial, legal, marital, family, health, and professional damages caused by these diseases. Healing must therefore be holistic and transcendent if it is to be rapid enough to justify the pursuit. Most of those who have recovered and whose lives are marked by freedom, serenity, and joy have found it necessary and practical to seek powers greater than themselves. They started by believing in believing. Soon that one-too-many believings faded away and faith banished fear. Maybe faith in God but, if not, then at least faith in the possibilities of life and the potential and worth of self. That's the magic: recovery believed in is recovery begun.

A Proven Pathway

Millions of C.D. people have found a practical pathway to spirituality in the Twelve Steps of Alcoholics Anonymous. A.A. is the unchallenged fountainhead from which has flowed our stubborn national acceptance of alcoholism as a treatable disease. Scott Peck, author of the immensely popular *The Road Less Traveled*, ranks A.A. among the three most important innovations of this century, along with television and the jet airplane. And deservedly so. He does this because the entire concept of self-help began with A.A. A.A. has saved more individual alcoholic lives and families than everything else ever tried combined. The famous Twelve Steps upon which the program is based has been adapted successfully as a remedy for just about every compulsive behavior known. There is little doubt that the treatment of alcoholism would still be in the Dark Ages were it not for the work of influential alcoholics who first found sobriety through this magnificent program. Marty Mann, author of *New Primer on Alcoholism* and the late founding president of the National Council on Alcoholism, herself recovered in A.A., states: "NCA was founded in 1944 in an atmosphere of total darkness. The public attitude was compounded of ignorance, fear, prejudice and hostility and the public attitude included most professionals. Almost nothing was being done about alcoholism except by alcoholics themselves."

A.A. at Work

Early employee assistance programs in major corporations such as Du Pont, Eastman Kodak, Standard Oil, and Consolidated Edison were simply based on referring employees with drinking problems to A.A. There was no other help available. In many cases these EAPs, as they later came to be known, were started and managed by employees who had found their own recovery in Alcoholics Anonymous. Most early treatment programs were simply medically supervised detoxification followed by introduction to this program.

Respected treatment centers to this day use the Twelve Steps and involve the patient in A.A. as the core of their program models. The Twelve-Step programs can be the bedrock of continued growth. And the gateway to adding a spiritual dimension to life.

Gather With the Strong

As you pursue intervention and recovery for your family, there will be no shortage of doubters, doomsayers, and providers of conflicting advice. Almost everyone around you will have had some experience with C.D. people—most of it painful and reflective of inaccurate information about the disease. Thus, it is important to rally around those who can offer encouragement, helpful input, and emotional support. You'll need friends to call when there is crisis or doubt, or when you want to share feelings and test out ideas. Support groups such as Al-anon, Alateen, Tough Love Parents, and Adult Children of Alcoholics are a readily accessible place to connect with such friends.

If self-help is not enough for you, then seek out a good professional therapy group to meet your needs. Perhaps a church in the community may be enlightened about C.D., offering an opportunity to meet people who are dealing with these same problems. But, by whatever means, it's crucial to find those from whom you can derive courage and strength. Co-dependency undermines the choice-making apparatus, so you will need encouragement to take the steps required. Living with a C.D. person's defensive behavior brings paralyzing guilt and fear. Thus breaking out of that trap is difficult without prompting and urging from concerned others. Most find that they need coaches, cheerleaders, and fellow team members to help them get moving. If you reach out to make these contacts, they will happen. As the Buddhists say, "When the student is ready, the teacher appears."

The Strength of Many

Chemical dependency and co-dependency can make their victims feel isolated and alone, as if these events and this pain were unique and never happened to anyone else. It has. In ten thousand years of Western culture probably no tragedy, even the frightening wars and plagues, has caused more pain. All around you—at work, in your neighborhood, and at church—are those who have recovered and those still suffering. Far from alone, you are standing in the midst of an enormous resource of recovery experience and shared pain. All you need to do is reach out...ask...step forward...seek and you really shall find. Your strength will be multiplied. Wellness can begin for you and your family right now. Use the guidelines suggested and find the help you need. And when the magic of intervention, treatment, and spiritual living has turned your pain to joy, look to those still suffering and do what you can to perpetuate the gift. Help the others still suffering to get help.

Resources

Organizations

The status of helpful resources for problems relating to alcohol and other drugs is ever-changing. Organizations and services evolve under the impact of media emphasis, level of public concern, health insurance trends, legislative changes, availability of funds, and a host of other variables. The following organizations have demonstrated a measure of staying power. Nonetheless, you may experience an occasional returned letter or disconnected telephone. Don't be discouraged. Try another, and you will no doubt eventually connect with the help needed.

A.A. World Service (Alcoholics Anonymous)
P.O. Box 459, Grand Central Station
New York, NY 10163
(212) 870-3400

Al-Anon/Alateen/Adult Child Family Groups
Headquarters
P.O. Box 862, Midtown Station
New York, NY 10018-0862
(800) 344-2666

A.A., Al-Anon, and Alateen are usually listed in the telephone directory. Call for meeting schedules and literature, or to talk to a member.

American Society of Addiction Medicine, Inc.
5225 Wisconsin Ave. NW, #409
Washington, DC 20015
(202) 244-8948

Many of the following national organizations may have local chapters in your community. Check the business pages in the telephone directory.

National Black Alcoholism & Addictions Council
1629 K St. NW, Suite 802
Washington, DC 20006
(202) 296-2696

National Clearinghouse for Alcohol and Drug Information (NCADI)
P.O. Box 2345
Rockville, MD 20847-2345
(301) 468-2600, (800) 729-6686

National Council on Alcoholism and Drug Dependency (NCADD)
12 West 21st St., 8th Fl.
New York, NY 10010
(212) 206-6770, (800) NCA-CALL

Council on Alcoholism/Drug Abuse
Listed in local telephone directory.

State Commission on Alcoholism/Drug Abuse
District offices are listed in local telephone directory.

Cocaine Hotline
1-800-COCAINE

Narcotics Anonymous
(818) 780-3951

Books

Alcoholics Anonymous. New York, NY: A.A. World Services, 1976.
The famous "Big Book" upon which A.A. and other twelve-step programs are based.

Twelve Steps and Twelve Traditions. New York, NY: A.A. World Services, 1953.
A timeless articulation of the foundational principles of the A.A. program.

The Dilemma of the Alcoholic Marriage. New York, NY: Al-Anon Family Group, 1981.
The official Al-Anon book about alcoholism, communication, and marriage.

Johnson, Vernon. *I'll Quit Tomorrow.* New York, NY: Harper & Row, 1973.
An explanation of the progressive disease of chemical dependency and ways to intervene, by the pioneer of the family intervention technique.

Mann, Marty. *New Primer on Alcoholism.* New York: Holt, Rinehart and Winston, 1950.

Classic by a pioneering woman founder of the National Council of Alcoholism.

Peck, M. Scott. *The Road Less Traveled*. New York, NY: Simon and Schuster, 1983.
Longtime best-seller about truth, reality, mature love, and successful living in the contemporary world.

Perkins, William Mack, and Nancy McMurtrie-Perkins. *Raising Drug-Free Kids in a Drug-Filled World*. Center City, MN: Hazelden, 1986.
Proven prevention guidelines for parents by two nationally recognized chemical dependency counselors.

Powell, John. *Fully Human, Fully Alive*. Niles, IL: Argus Communications, 1976.
Uplifting reflections on human worth, positive living, the significance of individuals, and the spiritual meaning of life.

Satir, Virginia. *Peoplemaking*. Palo Alto, CA: Behavior Books, 1972.
Thoughts about family systems and how they work by the revered originator of many of today's family therapy approaches.

Satir, Virginia. *Self-Esteem*. Palo Alto, CA: Science and Behavior Books, 1975.
A wonderful little book with profound meaning. A gift to yourself.

Woititz, J. *Adult Children of Alcoholics*. Pompano Beach, FL: Health Communications, 1983.
Describes self-defeating behaviors that are common to adult children of alcoholics and suggests what to do about them.

York, Phyllis, David York, and Ted Wachtel. *Toughlove*. Garden City, NY: Doubleday, 1982.
Help for parents dealing with rebellious adolescents.

For the Professional

NIAAA Dept. of Health and Human Services Public Health Service, Alcohol Drug Abuse & Mental Health Administration. *Alcohol Alert*. Rockville, MD 20857.

NIAAA Superintendent of Documents, US Government Printing Office. *Alcohol Health and Research World*. Washington, DC 20402. (202) 783-3238.

Quarterly.

Manisses Communication Group. *Alcoholism & Drug Abuse Week.* 3
    Govenor St., Providence, RI 02906-0357. (401) 831-6020.
Weekly on insurance, treatment, and legislative issues.

Index

Council on Alcoholism/Drug
   Abuse, 50, 52, 165-166, 175
Counselors, *See* Helping
   professionals
Criminal justice system. *See* Law
   enforcement
Crisis-based intervention
      cooperation with law
         enforcement, 78-79
      definition of, 70
      key elements of, 77-78
      medical crisis, 79-80
      techniques for, 82
      timing of, 77-78

Doctors, *See* Physicians
Domestic violence. *See* Violence
Drinking. *See* Alcohol use and
   abuse; Alcoholism; Chemical
   dependency
Drug dependency. *See also*
   Chemical dependency; War on
   Drugs
      historical cycle of drug
         experimentation, 149
      statistics on, 139, 150
Drug use and abuse. *See also* War
   on Drugs
      compared with alcohol use
         and abuse, 146, 148
      cycle of, 149
      dangers of, 146
      deaths from, 148
      statistics on, 144, 150
Dual diagnosis, 137-138

Employee assistance programs,
   55-56, 81, 88, 173
Employers. *See* Workplace
Enabling professional, 33

Families. *See also* Co-dependency
      children's experiences in
         C.D. families, 22-24
      co-dependency in 17-25, 28
      denial of feelings and anger,
         21-22

need to stop enabling, 25-26
parents of chemically
   dependent offspring, 28-29
reactions to concerned group
   intervention, 95-96
recovery from
   co-dependency, 72, 115-116
secrecy and, 27
support groups for, 27, 29,
   173-174, 175-176
violence in, 20
Family violence. *See* Violence
Ford, Betty, 137, 138

Group intervention. *See*
   Concerned group intervention

Healing. *See* Recovery; Treatment
Health care professionals. *See*
   Physicians
Health insurance. *See* Insurance
Health maintenance organizations,
   162
Helping professionals. *See also*
   Clergy; Physicians
      certification programs, 43
      chemical dependency of, 43
      co-dependency issues of,
         41-42
      concerned group
         intervention and, 94
      continuing education for, 34
      guidelines for selection, 51-52
      identification of effective
         professionals, 43
      lack of training in C.D.
         issues, 41, 42
      referrals from, 94
      termination of relationship,
         52
HMOs. *See* Health maintenance
organizations

Insurance, 34, 162, 170
Intervention
   as grief process, 69
   as martial art, 69

Some Other New Harbinger Self-Help Titles

The Headache & Neck Pain Workbook, $14.95
Perimenopause, $13.95
The Self-Forgiveness Handbook, $12.95
A Woman's Guide to Overcoming Sexual Fear and Pain, $14.95
Mind Over Malignancy, $12.95
Treating Panic Disorder and Agoraphobia, $44.95
Scarred Soul, $13.95
The Angry Heart, $13.95
Don't Take It Personally, $12.95
Becoming a Wise Parent For Your Grown Child, $12.95
Clear Your Past, Change Your Future, $12.95
Preparing for Surgery, $17.95
Coming Out Everyday, $13.95
Ten Things Every Parent Needs to Know, $12.95
The Power of Two, $12.95
It's Not OK Anymore, $13.95
The Daily Relaxer, $12.95
The Body Image Workbook, $17.95
Living with ADD, $17.95
Taking the Anxiety Out of Taking Tests, $12.95
The Taking Charge of Menopause Workbook, $17.95
Living with Angina, $12.95
PMS: Women Tell Women How to Control Premenstrual Syndrome, $13.95
Five Weeks to Healing Stress: The Wellness Option, $17.95
Choosing to Live: How to Defeat Suicide Through Cognitive Therapy, $12.95
Why Children Misbehave and What to Do About It, $14.95
Illuminating the Heart, $13.95
When Anger Hurts Your Kids, $12.95
The Addiction Workbook, $17.95
The Mother's Survival Guide to Recovery, $12.95
The Chronic Pain Control Workbook, Second Edition, $17.95
Fibromyalgia & Chronic Myofascial Pain Syndrome, $19.95
Diagnosis and Treatment of Sociopaths, $44.95
Flying Without Fear, $12.95
Kid Cooperation: How to Stop Yelling, Nagging & Pleading and Get Kids to Cooperate, $12.95
The Stop Smoking Workbook: Your Guide to Healthy Quitting, $17.95
Conquering Carpal Tunnel Syndrome and Other Repetitive Strain Injuries, $17.95
The Tao of Conversation, $12.95
Wellness at Work: Building Resilience for Job Stress, $17.95
What Your Doctor Can't Tell You About Cosmetic Surgery, $13.95
An End to Panic: Breakthrough Techniques for Overcoming Panic Disorder, $17.95
Living Without Procrastination: How to Stop Postponing Your Life, $12.95
Goodbye Mother, Hello Woman: Reweaving the Daughter Mother Relationship, $14.95
Letting Go of Anger: The 10 Most Common Anger Styles and What to Do About Them, $12.95
Messages: The Communication Skills Workbook, Second Edition, $13.95
Coping With Chronic Fatigue Syndrome: Nine Things You Can Do, $12.95
The Anxiety & Phobia Workbook, Second Edition, $17.95
Thueson's Guide to Over-the-Counter Drugs, $13.95
Natural Women's Health: A Guide to Healthy Living for Women of Any Age, $13.95
I'd Rather Be Married: Finding Your Future Spouse, $13.95
The Relaxation & Stress Reduction Workbook, Fourth Edition, $17.95
Living Without Depression & Manic Depression: A Workbook for Maintaining Mood Stability, $17.95
Coping With Schizophrenia: A Guide For Families, $13.95
Visualization for Change, Second Edition, $13.95
Postpartum Survival Guide, $13.95
Angry All the Time: An Emergency Guide to Anger Control, $12.95
Couple Skills: Making Your Relationship Work, $13.95
Self-Esteem, Second Edition, $13.95
I Can't Get Over It, A Handbook for Trauma Survivors, Second Edition, $15.95
Dying of Embarrassment: Help for Social Anxiety and Social Phobia, $12.95
The Depression Workbook: Living With Depression and Manic Depression, $17.95
Men & Grief: A Guide for Men Surviving the Death of a Loved One, $13.95
When the Bough Breaks: A Helping Guide for Parents of Sexually Abused Children, $11.95
When Once Is Not Enough: Help for Obsessive Compulsives, $13.95
The Three Minute Meditator, Third Edition, $12.95
Beyond Grief: A Guide for Recovering from the Death of a Loved One, $13.95
The Divorce Book, $13.95
Hypnosis for Change: A Manual of Proven Techniques, Third Edition, $13.95
When Anger Hurts, $13.95

Call **toll free, 1-800-748-6273,** to order. Have your Visa or Mastercard number ready. Or send a check for the titles you want to New Harbinger Publications, Inc., 5674 Shattuck Ave., Oakland, CA 94609. Include $3.80 for the first book and 75¢ for each additional book, to cover shipping and handling. (California residents please include appropriate sales tax.) Allow four to six weeks for delivery.

Prices subject to change without notice.